# TARRING

To Maurice and Lildear

with best wishes

Roger.

# TARRING

## A WALK THROUGH ITS HISTORY

ROGER DAVIES

TARRING

1990

First published 1990 in the United Kingdom by
Roger W Davies, The Hollies, 42 High Street Tarring, Worthing,
West Sussex BN14 7NR, from whom further copies may be obtained.



British Library Cataloguing in Publication Data
Davies, Roger *1946 Nov. 9-*
Tarring : a walk through its history.
1. West Sussex, history
I. Title
942.26

ISBN 0-9516309-0-3

Typeset in Palatino by Laser Images, Sandbach, Cheshire.

Printed by Hillman Printers (Frome) Ltd., Frome, Somerset.

*to Jane, with love*

# CONTENTS

# ILLUSTRATIONS

**Chapter 4**



**Chapter 5**



**Chapter 6**



**Chapter 7**

**Chapter 8**



**Chapter 9**



**Chapter 10**

**Chapter 11**



**Conclusion**

# ACKNOWLEDGEMENTS

I am grateful to the following for permission to reproduce photographs and other illustrations.

6, 9, 10, 11, 16a, 17, 18a, 19, 21a, 25, 34c, 35, 36, 37, 38a, 39a, 42a, 43, 44, 48, 49a, 51a, 52, 53, 59, 60a, 61a, 62a, 63, 65, 66, 68, 69, 70, 72, 74, 75, 76, 77, 81 and back dust jacket: Reproduced by kind permission of West Sussex County Council Library Service.

1: By courtesy of the West Sussex Record Office and the County Archivist.

2: Crown copyright. Reproduced with the permission of the Controller of Her Majesty's Stationary Office. IR 30/35/260.

4a,64a,71: Copyright 1990, Sussex Archaeological Society.

Reproduced from the Society's picture collections with the permission of the Society.

13a: Reproduced by kind permission of Frames of Broadwater.

24a,29,30,83,84: Reproduced by kind permission of Worthing Museum and Art Gallery.

45,56a: By courtesy of Messrs Strutt and Parker, owners of the original postcards, and the West Sussex Record Office, the custodians.

54a, 67a: Copyright Becket Newspapers. Pictures reproduced by kind permission of the Worthing Herald.

55: Reproduced by kind permission of Mr Daniel Shannon, Shannon Meats, South Street, Tarring, owner of the original photograph.

82,85,86,87: The Terry Child Postcard Collection. Reproduced by kind permission of Terry Child.

All other illustrations and all the modern photographs are from the author's collection.

# PREFACE

When our family first moved into The Hollies in Tarring High Street in 1981, we were intrigued by the date brick we found there. On an inside upstairs wall, it bore the initials R.& M.H., and the date 1774. The house appears to date from that time, but I was interested to know if I could discover the identity of what I assumed were the original owners.

Preliminary research in the Worthing Reference Library identified the occupiers of the house for the last hundred years, and for further information I was directed to the County Record Office at Chichester. There I was delighted to discover manor court rolls for Tarring, recording all the changes of ownership of most of the houses in the village, dating back to before the year in question. Tracing the ownership of the house back through the years, I eventually identified Richard and Mariah Hedgecock, R.& M.H., who owned the house in 1774. However, earlier documents described the house in identical terms, so it could not then have been a new building. Investigation of the structure of the house showed that underneath the Georgian facade was hidden a much older timber frame.

Looking back even further, I was confronted by records written in Latin. With only dim memories of school lessons, and an old and battered copy of "Teach Yourself Latin", interpretation was difficult, and to be sure I had the right records, I was forced to translate all the property transactions in the court rolls. When they were all transcribed, I soon realised that I was in possession of what was, to all intents and purposes, a full set of pieces of a gigantic jigsaw. Fitting all these pieces together was a job that took many months, but eventually, when the task was completed, I had constructed a complete picture of the ownership of the majority of the occupied sites in the village, from about 1650 to the present day.

Up until this point, my researches had been purely for my own interest, but I was able to give friends locally the histories of their own houses. Occasional snippets of information of more general interest, such as the location of the long lost pub called the Black Lion, made for good conversation at parties, and I soon found a wide variety of questions about the history of Tarring being directed at me. There were many stories of old Tarring which my researches had shown to be unreliable, and eventually, friends suggested that I should write a book!

My initial reaction was that although what I had found was of interest to owners of individual houses in the village, it was altogether too boring a collection of cold facts to provide material for a book, at least one that anyone would buy! I had also found the traditional local history format of "Domesday to the present" uninspiring, but I soon began to realize that there was much of interest to say about Tarring, and eventually I hit on the idea of an extended guide book, taking a leisurely walk through the village. This would include some of the more interesting facts about the individual houses, but could also digress into aspects of more general history as they affected our village.

In writing this book, I have received tremendous encouragement from many friends and associates. I am grateful to the staff of the County Record Office, for their enthusiastic help in guiding me through their records, and interpreting the occasional difficult Latin word. Special thanks are due to the staff at Worthing Library, and in particular to Martin Hayes, of the West Sussex County Council Library Service, who provided the facilities for me to make copies of many interesting photographs and drawings from the collection, and has kindly read and made valuable comments on the first draft of the book. I am also grateful to my many friends in Tarring for badgering me into writing the book in the first place, and for encouraging me to complete it. Finally, I would like to thank my wife, Jane, and my family. They have put up for almost two years with the clattering keys of my word processor, and a house full of photographs and manuscripts. Jane also undertook the laborious tasks of copy editing the text and compiling the index.

A book of this sort, while interesting to those who know and love the village, has a limited market, and it is difficult to find a publisher who will consider it a viable proposition to produce at a price most people can afford. I therefore decided to undertake the task myself. I have learned a lot on the way, but it would have been impossible without help from Ian and Miranda Howell of Laser Images who typeset the book from my text, and particularly from Mary Barnes of Hillman Printers, who guided me through the task of preparing copy for printing.

Every statement made in this book is based on a verifiable historical source: a number in square brackets indicates that a specific reference can be found on pages 201-206. Where no reference is given, the source is normally the manor court records or the Victoria County History of Sussex. However, there must be considerable further information about the history of the village hidden away in attics and family papers, and I would be very grateful to any reader who would be prepared to bring such material to my attention. In particular, I would welcome the opportunity to make copies of any old postcards, photographs or drawings which might enhance a future edition of this book.

For those who are interested in the detail of my original research, full copies of the text, entitled "The Copyhold Tenements of West Tarring, 1650-1900" have been deposited in Worthing Reference Library and the West Sussex Record Office.

*Tarring, 1990* *Roger Davies*

# GLOSSARY

| | |
|---|---|
| appurtenance: | a barn, stable or other building attached to a property. |
| backside: | land immediately behind and belonging to a house. |
| bordar: | a low ranking tenant, who worked on the manor lands in return for the tenure of a cottage. |
| brasinium: | a brewhouse. |
| chantry: | a gift used to provide an income to pay a priest to sing masses, usually in remembrance of the donor. |
| church ale: | an occasion when ale was sold and drunk in the church to raise funds for the church. |
| copyhold: | a form of tenancy of property, where proof of ownership was in the form of a copy of the court roll where the tenancy was recorded. |
| cotman: | a tenant of a cottage and small plot of land. |
| croft: | a piece of enclosed land adjoining a house. |
| cross: | a crossroads. |
| custumal: | a record of the local laws, or customs, of a manor. |
| demesne: | manor lands held directly by the lord. |
| enfranchisement: | the conversion of a copyhold tenancy into freehold. |
| franklin: | a freeholder of land in the manor. |
| glebe: | land belonging to the church, providing an income for the local priest. |
| healed: | roofed. |

| | |
|---|---|
| heriot: | a fine, generally the best beast, paid to the lord of the manor on the death of a tenant. |
| hide: | a measure of land, about 120 acres, originally supposed to be sufficient to support a family. |
| hovel: | a small, lowly dwelling-house, but not in the derogatory sense in which the word is used today. |
| lychgate: | a roofed gateway to a churchyard under which the corpse is set down at a funeral, to await the clergyman's arrival. |
| mercer: | a dealer in cloth. |
| messuage: | a dwelling house and associated buildings. |
| pannage: | the right to graze pigs in woodland. |
| pound: | an official enclosure for keeping stray cattle. |
| Rape: | one of the six Norman divisions of Sussex. |
| reredos: | a stone or brick section in the wall of a timber-framed house, against which a fire could be lit on an open hearth, or, a decorated screen behind an altar. |
| staple: | an export clearing house, where excise duties were levied. |
| tenement: | a house, with or without land. |
| terrier: | an ecclesiastical record of land holdings. |
| Terring(e)(s): | alternative early spellings of Tarring. |
| tithe: | a tax of one tenth of the value of the produce of land, payable to the Church. |
| twitten: | a Sussex word for a narrow footpath. |
| villein: | a villager obliged to stay in the village and work on the manor lands. |
| virgate: | a measure of land of uncertain size. |
| widow's bench: | the right of a wife to retain a tenancy in her husband's house after his death. |

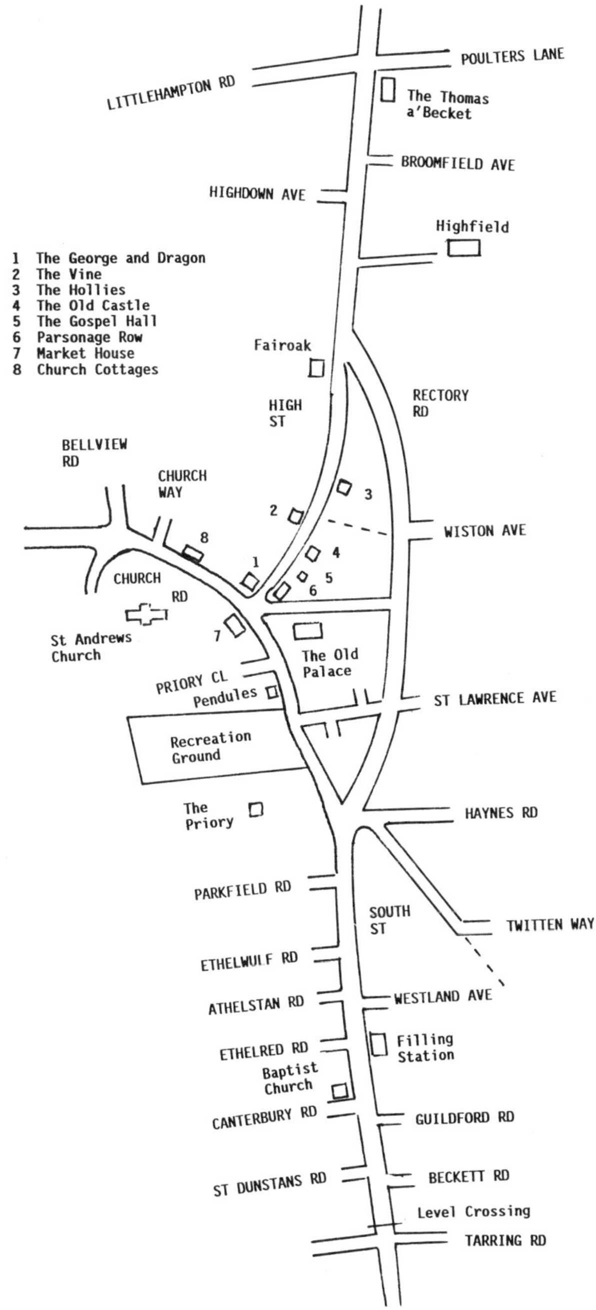


*The village of Tarring today.*

# INTRODUCTION

Tarring is an ancient village. It is mentioned in the Domesday book, compiled just 20 years after William the Conqueror landed along the coast at Pevensey, when there were 41 working men in the village. The earliest reference to the village is in around the year 939 when King Athelstan granted land here to the Church of Canterbury.

Numerous references to Thomas a'Becket, or more correctly St Thomas Becket, can be found in and around present day Tarring. Although there is no direct evidence that he ever visited the village, the church here has always been controlled directly by the Archbishop of Canterbury, rather than by the Bishop of Chichester as is the case with almost all other local parishes. Bishops and archbishops visited the parishes in their gift regularly and such a visitation is recorded by the archbishop in 1215. Becket died in 1170.

There is also a record, though possibly not reliable, that Archbishop Baldwin visited Tarring in 1189, when the monks here applied to know whether they might be permitted to go to the King, and return in safety [1].

No records of individual buildings in Tarring go back anything like this far. The Old Palace dates in parts from the thirteenth century and Parsonage Row probably from the fifteenth. There is, however, considerable documentary evidence relating to the history and occupancy of buildings in the village going back to around 1640, and it is from these sources that much of the information in this book has been obtained.

The most important by far are the records of the lord of the manor. At the time of the Domesday survey, the land in each manor fell into two categories. The first was land granted to free tenants, and their legal right to the land was the freehold ownership of English law. The rest of the land belonged to the lord of the manor, and was known as the demesne. It was cultivated by labourers, who could not leave the manor, and their service was obligatory, having its origins in the ancient concept of serfdom. These labourers, or villeins, were allowed to cultivate sections of the demesne land for their own use.

The black death, or bubonic plague, first arrived in the south of England in 1348, spread rapidly, and raged through the summer of 1349. It decimated the population, and although no figures survive for Tarring, it is likely that one in every two or three inhabitants of the village succumbed to this terrible affliction over the following fifteen years. Tarring survived this catastrophic event, but many similar villages were completely wiped out.

In this environment, there was a serious shortage of able-bodied men to work on the land. The lords attempted to reinstate debts of service, some of which had been replaced with cash payments in the twelfth century, but in the circumstances it was an impossible task, and only hastened the demise of the system. The obligation on workers to remain within the manor also became unenforceable, as lords competed for the scarce labour resources, and even laws passed in an attempt to limit the wages paid to labourers were ineffective. As a result, the balance of power in the relationship between the lord and his workers changed irrevocably in favour of the workers.

Whereas previously a villein's occupation of land had been at the will of the lord, it was more and more being recognised that the lord's power in this was not absolute. To begin with, the system conformed to previous custom and precedent, but gradually it became enshrined in law.

The system was controlled by the court baron, or manorial court, an assembly of the free tenants of the manor as judges and upholders of local law. In matters relating to the tenants in villenage, the court was known as the customary court, and its records, or court rolls, became the method whereby the customs of the manor were recorded as the real property law of the manor.

The proof of title to land was a written copy of the entry in the court roll granting it, and hence a tenancy of this sort was described as *held by copy of the court roll,* or copyhold.

The original copyhold tenancies retained much of the concept of villenage, and tenants were required to work on the demesne lands for specified periods in return for their tenancies. The lord was entitled to a payment in kind called a heriot, normally his best beast, on the death of a copyhold tenant, and although such tenancies could be passed on to succeeding generations, a fee had to be paid by the incoming tenant.

The complex rules or customs for each manor were set down from time to time in documents called custumals. Some examples from the Tarring custumal of around 1282 give a real flavour of the working relationship between copyhold tenants and the lord [2], and already begin to show signs of the slow transition from work services to cash payments which was taking place and was to continue over the next few centuries, considerably accelerating with the arrival of the black death.

Twenty holders of substantial pieces of customary land, each averaging almost a virgate [3], an uncertain measure of about twenty five acres, are listed, paying a rent of 15d per virgate four times a year. As an alternative, they could pay with personal work as follows:

> *And each one holding a half-virgate must reap ½ acre of wheat, 1 rood of barley and 1 rood of oats, he shall bind it up and bring it in. He shall carry ½ cartload of wood of Marlpost* (near Horsham) *and shall make two bushels of malt. And if the lord be in the vill, on his departure each tenant of 1 virgate shall do carrying service with one horse, and the others according to their holding more or less, to the lodging where he shall spend the night. He shall draw out dung with one cart until it is all carried away, and after the drawing out of the dung the lord shall give to the customers a feast and 2 men shall come from each virgate. He owes suit of court, and when he dies the lord shall have the best beast except a horse for heriot, and his wife shall pay relief at the term of St Thomas the Apostle, and she shall hold the tenement. He cannot marry himself, his sons or daughters without leave, and when his heir receives that tenement he shall give for relief a whole year's rent.*

Walter Cacher, one of six cotmen or cottagers, was a lesser mortal. He held a cottage and 2½ acres and owed:

> *From Michaelmas until Lammas for 42 weeks,except for the three holy weeks Christmas, Easter and Whitsun, 84 works, every week 2 works. And he shall thresh for 1 work 2 bushels of wheat, ½ seam of barley, 2 bushels of peas, 2 bushels of beans or 2 bushels of vetches or 1 quarter of oats for 1*

*work. He shall assist at the dung-heap when it is drawn out without counting it as a work. And after Lammas until St Matthew's Day he shall mow on every working day except Saturdays, on which no work is owed, ½ acre of any kind of corn; and between St Matthew's Day and Michaelmas he owes 2 works for the 1 week. And he shall gather ½ rood of stubble for 1 work, and he and the other cotmen with the oxherds shall have of the lord at Christmas, Easter and Midsummer 9 leaps* (a dry measure) *of barley of which 12 make 1 seam making a total of 18 bushels of corn. And he with the other cotmen and oxherds in harvest, shall have of the lord's corn 1 acre of wheat from the last 40 days and 1 acre of barley. And he shall give for heriot the best beast or 6d if there be none. And a work, outside harvest, is valued at ½d.*

The last sentence suggests that, during harvest at least, the work was obligatory, and payment in lieu not acceptable.

One work represented roughly a day's labour, so 84 works and some other services represented about one quarter of his available time. While this may seem a large proportion, there is an interesting parallel in the rule of thumb used by building societies seven hundred years later, that a mortgage should commit a borrower to a maximum of one quarter of his income.

The customs were restated [4] in 1577, by which time services and payments in kind, except for heriots, had largely been replaced by cash. Heriots continued to be seized until at least 1728, and in 1726 one copyholder was still paying 4 shillings and a cock in yearly rent.

The 1577 custumal describes the rights of copyhold tenants that prevailed unaltered until the abolition of copyhold tenures in the present century:

*1st. That time out of mind the memory of man is not to the contrary, the tenants of the said manor, by copy of Court Roll, hath done and ought to do their suit and service to the Lord's Court, and that they ought to pay such rents as in the ancient rentals are specified or are otherwise due and accustomed, and for their duties as in the said rental is particularly manifest and does there appear.*

*2nd. And if any tenant by copy of Court Roll of the Manor aforesaid shall purchase any lands or tenements of any such tenant that the purchaser shall pay a fine at the Lord's will, and he that shall surrender shall pay a heriot his best living beast.*

*3rd. And that 5 acres and above ought to pay a heriot, as appears in their former copies; and if it be not expressed in their old copies, that then less than 5 a. ought to pay five shillings in the name of a heriot after the death of every tenant dying thereof seized.*

*4th. And that every tenant aforesaid, who shall make or devise several surrenders (to wit) shall surrender one yard land to divers persons above 5 acres, the said tenant ought to pay several heriots as aforesaid (to wit) their best living beast.*

*5th. And if any such tenant shall die seized, that his youngest son, or if he shall have no son, his youngest daughter shall be his heir to all the land, tenements, cottages and underwoods whereof such tenant died seized, and if he shall have neither son nor daughter, that then the next of his blood shall inherit the lands and tenements aforesaid, in the manor aforesaid.*

*6th. And if any tenant will let on lease his customary or copyhold land or tenements, or any part thereof, that then every such tenant shall come to the Lord's Court and there in full and open court shall ask a license of the steward for the time being, to let, to farm the premises, or any part thereof, for so many years, as he shall please to let the same, and the steward ought to grant him such license, paying the Lord a fine for every year, 4d sterling.*

*7th. And that the tenants, by copy of Court Roll, hold their lands and hereditaments to them and their heirs in ancient fee, and not at the will of the Lord, but then only according to the custom of the manor, and that their copies are or ought to be so made.*

*8th. And if any tenant aforesaid shall die, his next heir shall come to the next Court to be holden for the said manor, and there ought to be admitted to all the lands, tenements and hereditaments whatsoever of which such tenant died seized, paying the Lord only a relief according to the ancient rent; that is to say, so much as it pays by the year, and for duty nothing.*

*9th. And every tenant of the manor, by copy of Court Roll, who holds one, two, three, four, or more tenements or yard lands, and dies seized of the premises, that such tenant ought to pay for the premises only one heriot, and for every cottage, or anything under a cottage, for heriot and relief, according to the old copies, and if it be not expressed in the old copies, that then they ought to pay as aforesaid.*

*10th. And if any such tenant shall die, the heir being under age, then the mother of such heir, or the father, if the inheritance descended from the mother, shall have the guardianship as well of the body as of the lands and tenements of such heir, until he shall attain the age of fifteen years freely, without paying any fine for the same; and after that the heir shall come to such age, that then he ought to be admitted to his lands and tenements to his own proper use and behoof.*

*11th. And if such heir shall have neither father nor mother, that then the next blood to such heir, and the furthest from the inheritance, shall have the minority of such heir, and that such heir, when he shall arrive at the age of fourteen years, may choose him his guardian, if his father be dead, or his mother betrothed to a husband.*

*12th. And lastly, that the relict of any tenant who shall die seized of any such state of inheritance, shall be admitted to her widow's bench freely, without anything to be paid therefor, and who ought to hold the same as long as she shall live chaste and unmarried; and that the heir during that time shall claim nothing out of the premises.*

Custom 5, granting natural inheritance to the youngest son rather than the eldest, is known as the custom of Borough English, and while unusual, was found more commonly in Sussex than elsewhere. It is thought to have its origins in Saxon customs, and it is probable that it was the normal rule prior to 1066, when the Norman custom of descent through the eldest son began to be generally imposed. The fact that Borough English prevailed in this county long after the Norman conquest, demonstrates the tenacity with which the South Saxons of Sussex clung to their independence.

The rule, which has a certain logic in ensuring that inheritance passed to the child least able to provide for himself, ensured that customs 10 and 11, dealing with inheritance by minors, were regularly applied. After 1700, it became increasingly common to override this provision by depositing a copy of the tenant's will with the court. In these circumstances the court was obliged to accept transfer in accordance with the will in preference to custom.

The requirement of custom 12 that a widow should remain chaste while she occupied her widow's bench was taken seriously, and besides numerous instances of properties being given up on remarriage of widows, a widow, Mary Tate, forfeited her small cottage in High Street to her son in 1803 for having a child born out of wedlock. The evidence would have been hard to deny, since her husband died in 1800!

Transactions relating to copyhold tenancies were dealt with at regular meetings of the manor court, and the proceedings were recorded in the manor court rolls [5], which were, in fact, manuscript books. The village of Tarring was the major settlement in a manor called "West Tarring with Marlpost"; West to distinguish it from East Tarring, or Tarring Neville, in East Sussex. Marlpost is a district south of Horsham where the manor owned woodlands. We are fortunate in Tarring that the court rolls have been preserved without break from 1638 to the present century, and they can be examined at the County Record Office in Chichester. Since they record transactions in land, the rolls naturally have to describe the property concerned well enough for it to be identified in the event of a dispute, and they thus provide us with a valuable record, not only of the ownership of land, but also of the nature of the buildings, particularly as most of the houses in the village were built on copyhold land.

The earliest volumes are written in Latin and a system of abbreviations makes interpretation somewhat difficult. There is a short period of surprising lucidity, however, starting in 1651 when the scribe suddenly changes to a very legible English handwriting, reflecting the influence of Oliver Cromwell during the interregnum following the execution of King Charles I. However the respite is short lived and by 1660 the scribe has reverted once more to mediaeval Latin, very promptly reflecting the restoration of the monarchy under Charles II.

The record continues in Latin until 1728 when it finally reverts to English. This was not before time. With increasing regularity in the years leading up to that date, the scribe was defeated by the problem of translating everything into Latin, and increasingly used English words instead.

After 1841, a succession of Acts of Parliament provided for the conversion of copyhold tenancies to freeholds, a process called enfranchisement, and in 1922 they were finally abolished.

Besides the service and fines owed by inhabitants to the lord of the manor, the system of tithes operated whereby one tenth of all that was produced from the land was due to the church. After 1836 the Tithe Commutation Acts provided for the replacement of the levy in kind by a cash payment. The Tithe Commissioners only fixed the total due from each parish, and it remained for the parish to apportion the charge to the individual landowners. Since the charge related to the area of land occupied, and the resulting apportionment had to be recorded, the process necessitated the accurate mapping of the village.

A copy of the tithe apportionment map of Tarring dated about 1839 is preserved in the Public Record Office in Kew [6].It is a document of impressive proportions, and shows every house, barn, outbuilding and field in the village, each with a reference number. An accompanying book lists for each reference the nature of the property, its owner and its occupier.

These days we think of Tarring as the village itself with a few surrounding streets, although estate agents often seem to take a much wider view. The parish in 1839 was considerably more extensive. The central section was roughly a square bounded by Littlehampton Road in the north, Ringmer Road extended southwards in the west, the railway line in the south, and a line running north from the railway footbridge in Pavilion Road to the east. The area was substantially increased, however by three additional "tongues" of land extending to the north, south and west.

The western extension included the area between Terringes Avenue, Palatine Road and the Littlehampton Road, to where the two roads meet at the Yeoman public house. To the south, the land

---

1. *This page from the court roll of 1641 records the surrender by James Evans to Thomas Bottinge of a mansion house with a barn, an orchard and a garden,* (The Hollies) *and also a virgate of customary land called Hampers* (a field to the east of the village). *A heriot of five shillings and James's best animal (optim aial) was noted in the margin.*

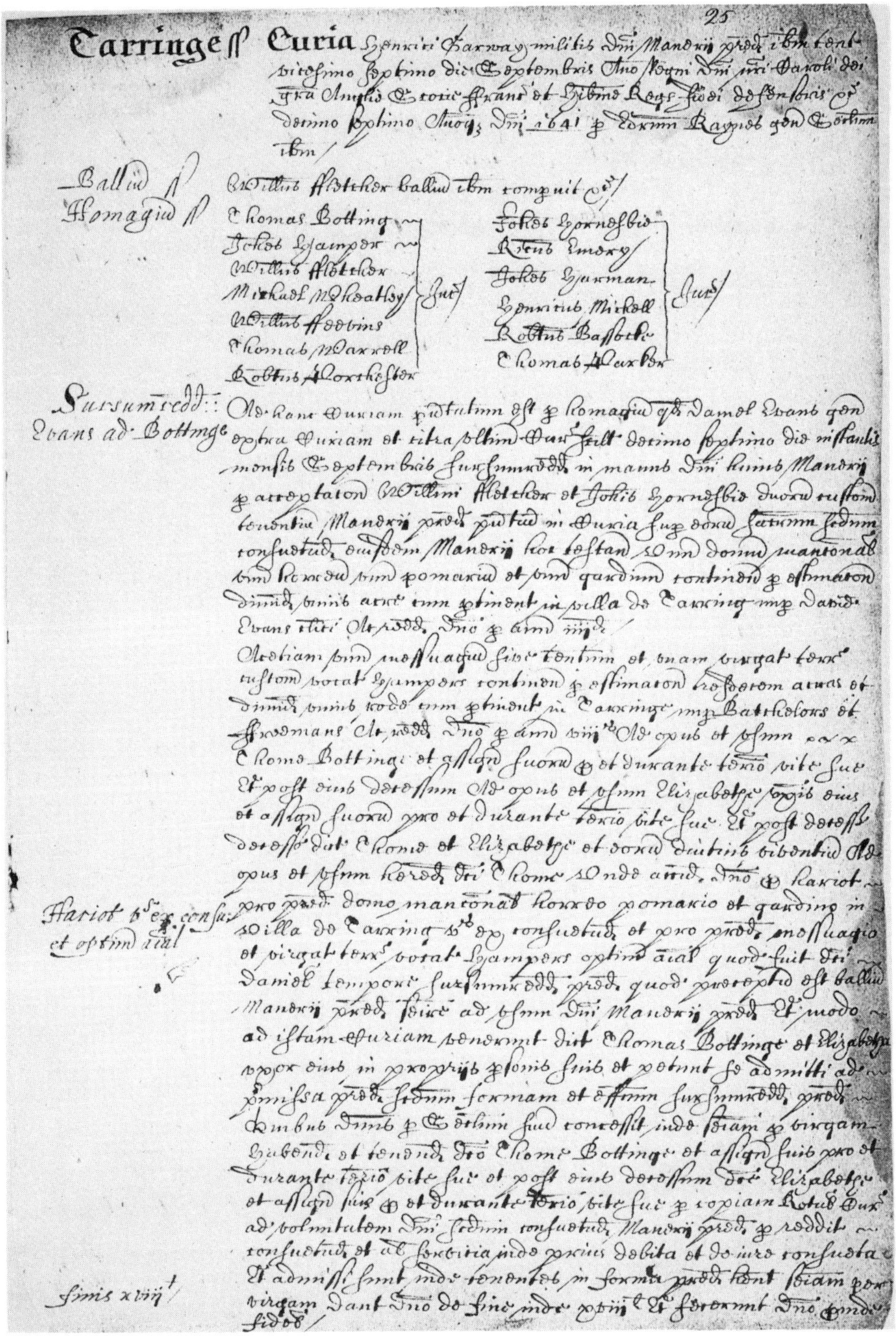
25

Carringe ss Curia Henrici Harvay militis dni Manerii pred ibm tent vicesimo septimo die Septembris Anno Regni dni nri Caroli dei gra Anglie Scotie Franc et Hibnie Regis fidei defensoris &c decimo septimo Annoqz Dni 1641 p Edrum Rayneb gen Senlm ibm /

Ballius ss Willus ffletcher ballius ibm compuit &c /

Homagiu ss

| | | | |
|---|---|---|---|
| Thomas Botting<br>Johes Hamper<br>Willus ffletcher<br>Michael Mchcathy<br>Willus ffebbins<br>Thomas Maxwell<br>Robtus Worchester | Jur / | Johes Hornebie<br>Ricus Emery<br>Johes Harman<br>Henricus Mickell<br>Robtus Bassett<br>Thomas Parker | Jur / |

Sursumredd: Evans ad Bottinge

Ad hanc Curiam psentatum est p homagiu qd Daniel Evans gen extra Curiam et citra ultim Cur tent decimo septimo die instantis mensis Septembris sursumredd in manus dni huius Manerii p acceptacon Willmi ffletcher et Johis Hornebie duoru custom tenentiu Manerii pred psentacu in Curia hac dcoru statum secdm consuetud eiusdem Manerii hoc testan Unu domu mancional unu horreu unu pomariu et unu gardinu continend p estimacon dimid unius acre cum ptinent in villa de Carring nup David Evans clici Ac redd Dno p annu iiijd /

Ac etiam unu mesuagiu sive tentum et unam virgat terr custom vocat Hampers continen p estimacon viginti acras et dimid unius redd cum ptinent in Carringe nup Batchelors et ffreemans Ac redd Dno p annu viijs Ad opus et usum ...x Thome Bottinge et assign suoru p et durante termo vite sue Et post eius decessum Ad opus et usum Elizabethe uxoris eius et assign suoru pro et durante termo vite sue Et post decess decess dict Thome et Elizabethe et doru diutius viventiu Ad opus et usum hered dci Thome Unde accid Dno p hariot

Hariot vd ex consu et optim aial

pro pred domo mancional horreo pomario et gardino in villa de Carring vd ex consuetud et pro pred mesuagio et virgat terr vocat Hampers optim aial quod fuit dci Daniel tempori sursumredd pred quod preceptu est ballio Manerii pred seire ad usum Dni Manerii pred Et modo ad istam Curiam venerunt dict Thomas Bottinge et Elizabetha uxor eius in propriis psonis suis et petunt se admitti ad pmissa pred secdm formam et effectum sursumredd pred Quibus eius p Senlm suu concessit inde seisiam p virgam Habend et tenend dco Thome Bottinge et assign suis pro et durante termo vite sue et post eius decessum dce Elizabethe et assign suis p et durante termo vite sue p copiam Rotul Cur ad voluntatem Dni secdm consuetud Manerii pred p reddit consuetud et al servitia inde prius debita et de iure consueta Et admissi sunt inde tenentes in forma pred hent seisiam per virgam dant Dno de fine inde xviijs Et fecerunt Dno fidel fidel /

ffinis xviijs /

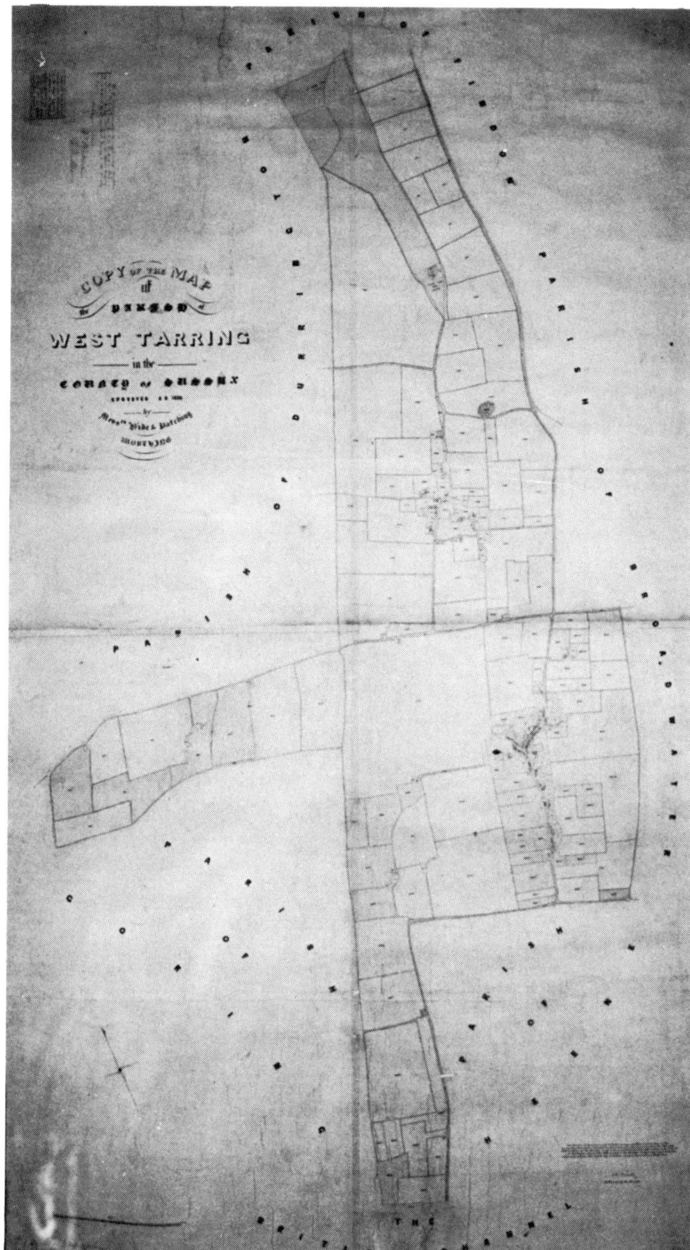


*2. The tithe map of Tarring, drawn in 1839. It is remarkably accurate, and every house, barn and field is numbered. The detail, right, shows the village centre.*

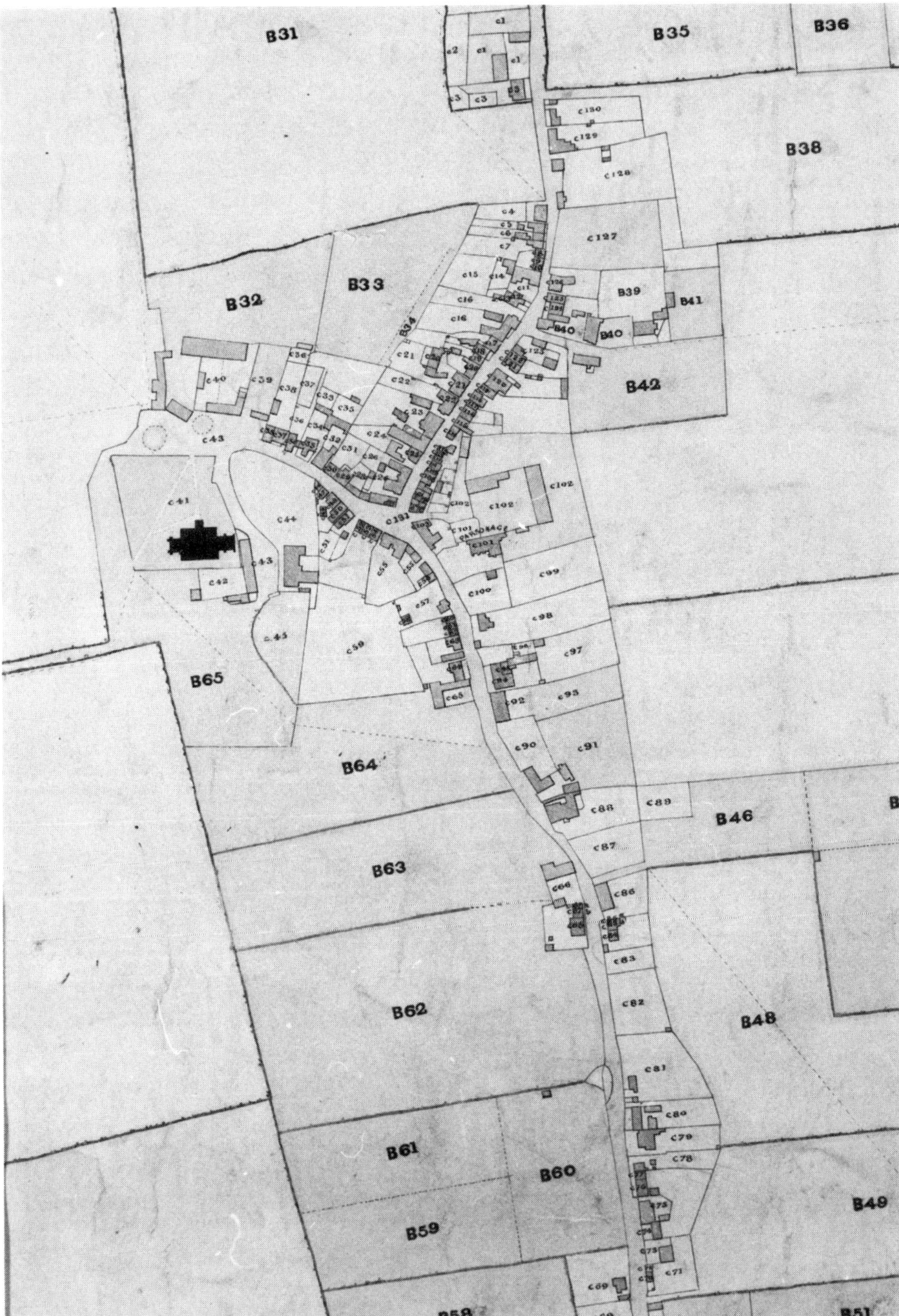
B31
B35
B36
B38
B32
B33
B34
B39
B41
B40
B42
c127
c128
c130
c129
c41
c44
c43
c42
c59
c100
c99
c98
c97
c92
c90
c91
c88
c89
c87
c86
c83
c82
c81
c80
c79
c78
c71
c69
c68
B65
B64
B46
B63
B62
B48
B61
B60
B59
B49
B58
B51

between Wallace and George V Avenues extended Tarring to the sea, an area called, appropriately enough, seafields.

The largest extension, to the north, extended northwards from the top of Ringmer Road to West Hill at the top of High Salvington, the site of the present BBC radio relay mast. The eastern boundary of this section is marked by the A24 and Offington Lane. The area contains the ancient village of Salvington, around the John Selden public house where a number of old buildings can still be seen. The overall shape of the parish, as a long thin strip including downland, coastal plain and seashore, is typical of parishes on the coast of Sussex, allowing inhabitants access to a variety of soil types to meet their different needs.

The windmill at the top of Salvington Hill is ideally situated, and the line of the medieval track to it from Salvington village can still be traced. Travelling north from the Selden it follows Half Moon Lane until it reaches the A27. Here it goes almost straight ahead, following the line of the modern road, until it turns sharply left and the track goes straight on into Mill Lane. Although this road deteriorates quickly, it is, in fact, passable with care by car and emerges eventually right next to the windmill at the top - a considerably more direct route than the present roads offer. From here, the track continues on over the Downs to Storrington. Until 1804, this was, in fact, the main road from Tarring to Storrington, giving some idea of the difficulties that travellers faced in those days.

The court rolls generally describe the position of a property by reference to adjacent ones, or to previous owners, but cross-referencing to the tithe map can provide a precise identification. In addition of course, the map provides the first indication of the outline shape of buildings in the village, which helps in differentiating between buildings which have been replaced and those which have simply been renovated.

---

*3. The parish, and the manor of Tarring, extended from the sea to the top of High Salvington. Until the last hundred years, the only settlements were in the village itself and the small village of Salvington, at what is now known as the Seldon.*

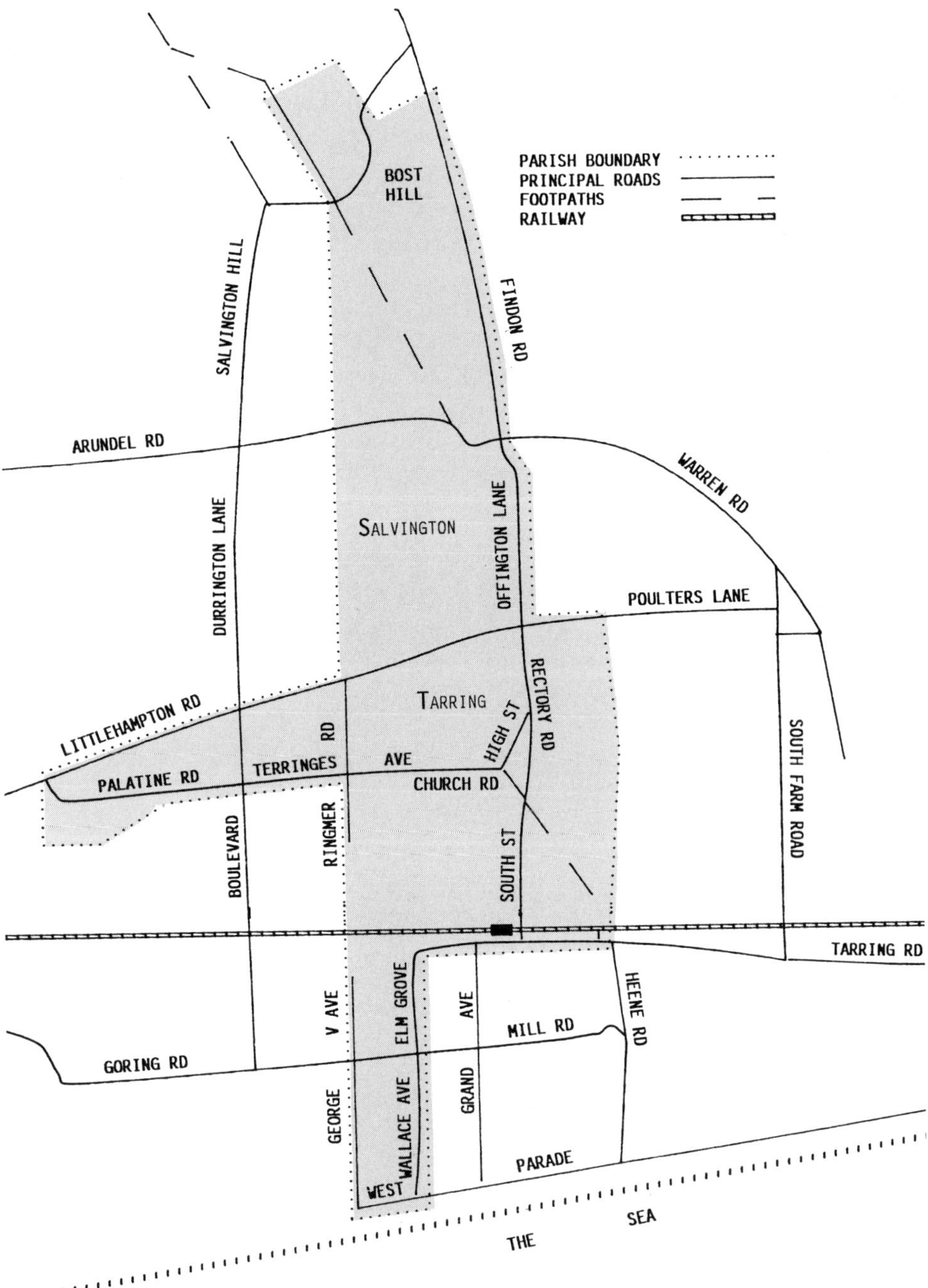
PARISH BOUNDARY
PRINCIPAL ROADS
FOOTPATHS
RAILWAY
BOST HILL
SALVINGTON HILL
FINDON RD
ARUNDEL RD
WARREN RD
DURRINGTON LANE
SALVINGTON
OFFINGTON LANE
POULTERS LANE
LITTLEHAMPTON RD
TARRING
RECTORY RD
HIGH ST
RD
PALATINE RD
TERRINGES AVE
CHURCH RD
SOUTH FARM ROAD
BOULEVARD
RINGMER
SOUTH ST
TARRING RD
ELM GROVE
AVE
HEENE RD
V AVE
MILL RD
GORING RD
GEORGE
WALLACE AVE
GRAND
PARADE
WEST
THE SEA

Further helpful information comes from the records of the levy of a tax on hearths [7] in 1662, and the land tax records from the eighteenth and nineteenth centuries [8]. The collection of local directories in Worthing Reference Library is a particularly valuable source for information on occupants of the village since 1850.

All these local history records provide an insight into the history of the houses in the village, which this book relates. It is laid out as a guided tour of the centre of the village of Tarring, and, as is traditional on such walks, we will navigate largely by reference to pubs! We begin at the George and Dragon, at the bottom of the High Street.

CHAPTER ONE

# THE GEORGE

In the reign of King Edward VI, in 1553, an Act of Parliament was passed laying down the principle of licensing of premises where alcohol was sold, a concept which has survived to the present day. The Act was entitled *An Acte to avoyde the greate price and excess of Wynes,* and in the words of its preamble, was intended *for the avoyding of many inconveniences muche evill rule and comune resorte of misruled persons used and frequented in many Taverns of late set uppe in very great noumbre in back lanes corners and suspicious places within the Cytie of London and in divers other Townes and Vyllages within this realm.*

Drunkenness and associated misbehaviour were obviously a problem at the time, and the Act was an attempt both to regulate the price of wine, and to limit the number of taverns from which it could be sold. It stipulated that taverns could only be kept in cities, towns, corporate boroughs, port towns and market towns, and that generally each such town should have no more than two taverns, although there were some listed exceptions. Fortunately for the inhabitants of Tarring at the time, it was then a market town, rather than the village it later became, and in 1597, a licence was granted [9] to Walter Crabbe of Tarring by none less than Sir Walter Raleigh, to sell wines retail.

Whether this tavern was situated on this site is not clear, although it seems likely, as certainly in 1610, Moses Brian owned a tavern here called the White Horse. As the only tavern in the village at the time, it would have been important as a meeting place and a stopping point for travellers.

To give some idea of the scarcity of such hostelries under the new law, in 1636 a guidebook to Sussex taverns [10] shows the nearest inns to Tarring's to be at Arundel in the west, Shoreham in the east, and Steyning in the north.

By 1643, a second tavern called the Ship had opened nearby, and ever since there have always been at least two public houses in the village. However, the George and Dragon is the only one with such a long continuous history. It remained the White Horse until 1781, when its name was changed to the George. It is first referred to by its present name of the George and Dragon in 1855.

It was an important coaching inn before the development of Worthing in the early nineteenth century, and with its attendant shops it must have been a focal point of village life. Manor courts were held there on occasions, but its main claim to a place in history must come from the many references to its alleged importance as a meeting place for smugglers.

It is generally thought that smuggling consisted of the importation of contraband alcohol and tobacco, but in fact for the greater part of its history, smuggling involved primarily the illicit export of wool [11]. Wool has played a central part in the economic history of England, recognised today in the woolsack on which the Lord Chancellor sits in the House of Lords.

The gradual transition from labour to cash in payment of manor rents in the thirteenth century led to a growing shortage of labour on demesne farms. The lords turned more and more from arable to sheep farming, since this was less labour intensive. In addition, tenants found that sheep wool, as a saleable commodity, was useful in generating the cash for the money payments. As a result, there was a major reduction in the amount of food produced in areas like Tarring, and over the country as a whole, there was not enough to feed the population. In an attempt to deal with this problem, the export of wool was forbidden in 1274.

There is a record of an illegal exportation of wool from Shoreham in that year, probably the first of many recorded instances of smuggling in this area. In 1275, export of wool was allowed on payment of a heavy excise duty, and this principle remained, interspersed with a number of periods of complete prohibition, until the war with France in 1793 which followed the commencement of the French Revolution.

With its proximity to the continent, and long stretches of barren coastline, constantly changing with the erosion of the sea, Sussex presented irresistible opportunities for smuggling, countered by regular attempts on behalf of the Government to stamp out this substantial drain on the Exchequer. In 1436, for instance, export of wool was restricted to shipments from specific wharfs to the staple, or

*4. The George and Dragon is the oldest public house in the village, and its history can be traced back to before 1610. The pencil drawing was made in 1869 by Sarah Winton Hide.*

clearing house, at Calais. This was, at that time, in English hands, following the famous victory of Henry V over the French at Agincourt in 1415. Exporters were required to bring back certificates of unloading, against a surety. This only further encouraged the evasion of duty.

From 1630, numerous proclamations forbade the export of wool at all, on penalty of death, but the practice was by then endemic, and continued unabated. The attempts at enforcing the law only served to ensure that the illicit cargoes were better protected by the smugglers, often using large bands of armed men. By 1671, Calais alone had imported forty thousand sacks of wool in the previous two years, and the trade was so valuable that it was well known that smugglers were able to evade capture and punishment by the widespread bribery of officials.

Despite further attempts at regulating the sale and purchase of any wool within fifteen miles of the Sussex coast, the trade continued vigorously, and indeed, the authorities' vain attempts to control it over a period of almost five hundred years bear a marked resemblance to trying to push water uphill! The trade finally came to an end, not as the result of effective law enforcement, but by the onset of yet another war with France.

In contrast to this long history of the illicit export of wool, recorded instances of illegal importation go back only to around 1700. In 1720, a custom-house officer had his horse shot from under him at Ferring in an encounter with over sixty armed men engaged in the smuggling of tea.

By 1763, the trade in alcohol was well established. A half-anchor was a cask of about four gallons, and sixty of them, full of brandy, were found by customs-house officers on the beach at Kingston, near Ferring [12]. It was alleged that the greater part of the four million gallons of Geneva gin distilled annually at Schiedam in Holland were smuggled into England. When you consider that this was the output of just one distillery, and the population of the whole country at that time was certainly no more than eight million, it gives some impression of the extent of the evasion of duty, and, incidentally, of the considerable volumes of gin being consumed in England at this time.

In the early years of the nineteenth century there were numerous bloody confrontations between smugglers and excise men, including one involving over two hundred men at Worthing in 1832. Smuggling of gin and brandy continued throughout the nineteenth century, and it was said that Worthing fishermen were still smuggling brandy from France in the 1920's.

There are persistent stories linking the men of Tarring, and particularly the George and Dragon, with this trade, and given its extent, it is unlikely that Tarring could have escaped an involvement of some sort. However, I can find no specific reference to date.

The vicar in 1860, although a rather unreliable source in some respects,wrote [13]:

*They were used to say here, that every other man you met was a Smuggler, - but it was a mild, soft sort of speech, for, in truth, there was no man, who, one way or another, was not concerned in some venture or another.*

As we shall see, the Miller of Highdown was at least favourably disposed towards smuggling, and in all probability used the sails of his windmill on Highdown Hill to signal to the smugglers. It has also been suggested that his tomb, constructed almost thirty years before he died, would have made an ideal hiding place for brandy and tobacco. There was also said to have been an empty tomb in the churchyard which was used for the storage of smuggled goods.

Ecclesden Manor, which lies on the western slopes of Highdown Hill, certainly had a secret shaft from the attic to a concealed entrance on the ground floor, and at least two further hiding places in the grounds, one cleverly constructed within the walls of a dovecote [14]. There are two natural paths from Tarring to the sea and the one through Heene can still be followed. It leads from the bottom of High Street to the junction of South Street and Rectory Road. From here it follows Twitten Way. Where the road veers to the left, a twitten, a Sussex name for a narrow footpath, leads straight ahead. It continues its diagonal path in a direct line to the top of Heene Road, ignoring the rectangular layout of the gardens of the much newer houses and roads, and crossing the railway by means of a footbridge. From here, the path follows Heene Road to the sea.

*5. The bottom of the High Street at the beginning of the the century. In the top illustration, the shop in Market House is George Fenner, Grocer, Draper and Outfitter, and the original facade of the malthouse can be seen on the right. The lower scene shows the small building which stood to the south of the George.*

The path to the west is now rather fragmented, but traces can still be found showing where it led from the south west corner of the churchyard diagonally to the footbridge over the railway at the top of Elm Grove. From here it led south, slightly to the west of Elm Grove and Wallace Avenue, to the sea.

It might have been considerably more prominent today if the plans developed in the 1930's for a ring road in the west of Worthing had come to fruition [15]. Some sections of the road were, in fact, built and still exist. Unfortunately, however, three key links were not completed, perhaps because of the intervention of the war.

The road began as a continuation of Marine Parade from where it previously ended at the border of old Tarring at the end of Wallace Avenue. This first section of the road is a dual carriageway. The road then continued north by way of George V Avenue, still an impressive road, and crossed the Goring Road at the George crossroads.

Further north, this road suddenly stops at a dead end. The original plans called for a new bridge over the railway at this point, and the road was to continue along Princess Avenue. Neither the northern junction of this road with St Andrews Road, nor the railway bridge were ever completed, leaving Princess Avenue stranded as a wide through road with nowhere to go through to at either end!

The road was to go from here by way of Pelham Road, which also shows the intention by its present width, to join the newly built Rectory Road at its junction with High Street. The construction of a new development between Pelham and Rectory Roads now blocks this route, and it seems unlikely that the proposal will ever be revived. A pity, since it would certainly relieve the traffic congestion at Tarring crossing.

The Heene path had a major disadvantage for the smuggler. The point at which it reached the sea was near the site of a watchtower built at the back of the beach, about seventy five metres east of the end of Wallace Avenue. Its purpose was to protect the coast from enemy attack during the war with France, 1702 to 1706, over the question of succession to the Spanish throne. By 1724, however, in the words of the court roll *since the Time of Building the said Watch House, the Sea hath gained on the Land, and driven the Beach over the Place, where the said Watch House stood*. It was later replaced by a naval signal post.

*6. The signal post at Heene, shown here in 1814, was built to replace the previous watchtower, which was destroyed by the sea. It communicated naval intelligence with similar posts along the coast using semaphore signals. The drawing clearly shows the low cliff that existed on the coast at the time, but was itself eventually swept away.*

The other path was a much better proposition, meeting the sea almost equidistant between the watchtowers of Heene and Kingston, and it must have been here that the smugglers of Tarring plied their trade. The association of this area with smuggling is preserved today in the street name of Smugglers Walk.

To return to the George: in 1828, as the days of the smuggler were appoaching their end, the inn was taken over by Richard Tamplin, a member of a famous brewing family whose beers can still be bought here today. It is thus an early example of a tied house.

The street in which the George stands is called High Street, but this was not always so. Originally there was only one street in Tarring, leading from what is now the railway crossing to the George, and continuing northwards. Before 1880, Glebe Road was simply a gate into the fields behind the parsonage, Rectory Road is only fifty years old, and Church Road was until relatively recently just a short lane leading from the market-place to the church and Church Farm.

Naturally, then, the whole of this street was known simply as the

Street of Tarring, or Tarring Street, with the section south from the market-place called the South Street, as it still is, and the northerly section the North Street. It was referred to as such in 1650, and still in 1879, although by 1851, the section from the George to the Vine was sometimes called High Street. By 1894, the whole of the northern section had become High Street.

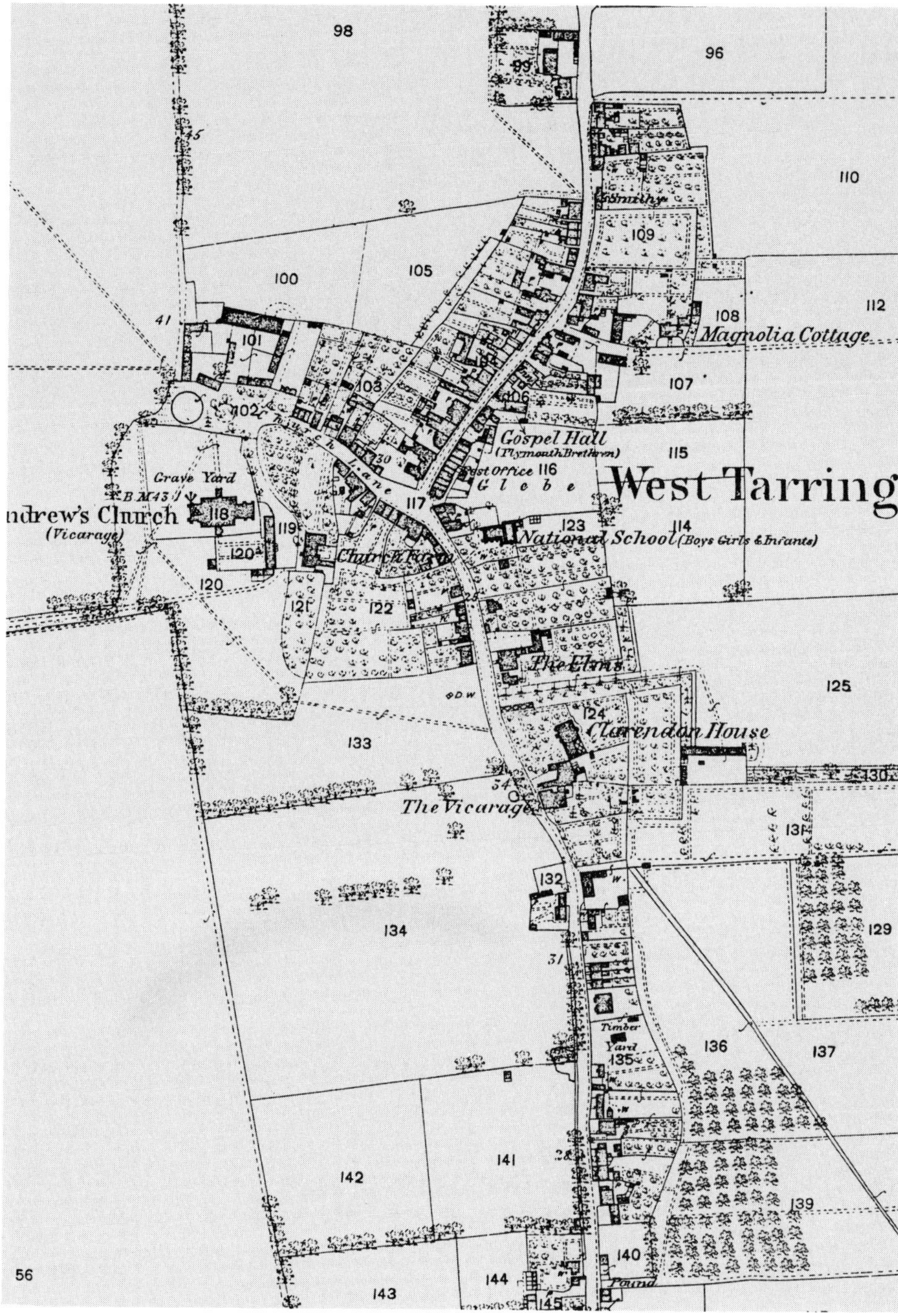

7. The village of Tarring in 1875.

CHAPTER TWO

# MALTHOUSE COTTAGE

The house that stood on the north side of the George in 1610, owned by William Wingfield, was called Naves, and it still bore that name 230 years later, when its tenant John Barker bought the freehold from the manor. John was an extensive landowner of the time, and we shall regularly come across pieces of his large but fragmented estate during our walk. The building that stands here today probably contains much of the fabric of the original structure of 350 years ago.

In 1675, the house was recorded as having just one hearth, and the barn then as now attached to the house was being used by Edward Gates as a smithy. Although this was very convenient for the owners of the many horses that visited the inn next door, it was very short lived, and the business was taken over by the two longer established smithies we shall discover farther up the street. By 1682, Edward had converted the barn for use as a malthouse, and this was still so in the nineteenth century. Edward Sayers took possession in 1721, and the property remained in the hands of the Sayers family until it passed to John Barker in 1801.

The making of malt is the essential first process in the production of ale. It involves soaking barley in water and spreading it out thinly over the floor of the malthouse to allow it to germinate. When the root appears and the grain begins to shoot, the malt is dried in a kiln to prevent further growth, and to give it the colour and flavour which it contributes to the final product.

Ale is produced by using yeast to induce fermentation in a mixture of malted barley, sugar and water. If hops are added to enhance the flavour, the resulting brew is called beer. Ale and beer have been produced for many thousands of years, and the process was known to the ancient Egyptians. However, it was originally produced at home for domestic consumption, and certainly at this time the White Horse next door would have been producing its own brew.

Until recently the cottage was known as Malthouse Cottage,

recalling the origins of the building, although it is unlikely that malt has been made here during the last hundred years. At the turn of the century, the storehouse to the north had a facade with a domestic front door and window, and this was replaced by the present barn doors subsequently, perhaps when the premises were used as a builders yard in around 1921. The premises have more recently seen service as an electrical engineers workshop, a garage and a storeroom.

The next building, which has been known for some time as Banner House, was part of a large tenement stretching up as far as number 19 High Street. While most holdings in Tarring in the seventeenth century and earlier were of a size which would seem very large today - there were only three on the west side of High Street from the George to the Vine - this one was particularly substantial. It contained three houses, of which this was one of the smaller two.

Banner House has been described as dating from the seventeenth century [16]. It is certainly at least as old as that, and may be considerably older. Excavations [17] were undertaken recently on land which was originally associated with the house, and is now the forecourt of Tarring Boys Club. Although there was little time for detailed investigation by members of the Sussex Archaeological Society, the remains of a plaster floor were found, and on it, fragments of pottery from the fourteenth century.

There are a few records of transactions concerning houses in Tarring from around this time. The earliest [18] dates from 1274 , when Simon of Salvington and his wife Ann bought a messuage in Terringes from John de la More for payment of an unmewed sparrowhawk. The house payed rent to the lord of one clove per year. Of course, we have no way of knowing where the house was situated.

The clove was a measure of wool equal to seven pounds weight. A mew was a cage used for confining hawks when they were moulting, and was an essential part of any substantial estate. The cages in London where the King's birds were kept stood on the spot where the royal stables were subsequently built, which accounts for the origin of the modern meaning of the word mews.

Before the sixteenth century, only the very rich built their houses of timber or stone. Such structures required the services of skilled craftsmen, and these were beyond the means of the ordinary man, who had to construct his own house as best he could. The resulting hovels were temporary structures which had to be replaced regularly, and none have survived to the present day.

The site of Banner House seems to have been part of really old Tarring, but all we can be sure of is that by 1650, the house had been here for some time. It is probably a product of what is known as "the great rebuilding", which lasted from 1550 to 1650, but reached its peak in the years between 1575 and 1625.

The restraints on the export of wool which led to the growth of smuggling in this area also stimulated the growth of a domestic industry in the processing of wool, and by the middle of the sixteenth century, England was a major exporter of cloth. As a result, the economy flourished, and it was this prosperity that produced the wealth to finance the great rebuilding. As a contemporary chronicler [19] put it:

> *In building, so well the hedge as the parke oke go all one waie, and never so much heth beene spent in a hundred years before, as in ten yeare of our time; for everie man almost is a builder, and he that hath bought any small parcell of ground, be it never so little, will not be quiet till he have pulled downe the old house (if anie were there standing) and set up a new after his owne devise.*

During this period, many of the older temporary houses in the village were replaced by more permanent structures built with a timber frame. These were constructed from oak, in contrast to the earlier houses, which used a variety of softer woods which, while easier to work, produced much less durable buildings. As our chronicler continued:

> *For albeit that there were then greater number of mesuages and mansions almost in everie place; yet were their frames so slight and slender, that one meane dwelling house in our time is able to countervaile verie manie of them, if you consider the present charge with the plentie of timber that we bestow upon them. In times past men were contented to dwell in houses, builded of sallow, willow, plumtree, hardbeame, and elme, so that the use of oke was in maner dedicated wholie unto churches, religious houses, princes palaces, noblemens lodgings, and navigation: but now all these are rejected and nothing but oke anie what regarded.*

*And yet see the change, for when our houses were builded of willow, then had we oken men; but now that our houses are come to be made of oke, our men are not onlie become willow, but a great manie...altogither of straw. In those the courage of the owner was a sufficient defense to keepe the house in safetie but now the assurance of the timber, double doores, lockes and bolts must defend the man from robbing. Now we have manie chimnies and yet our tenderlings complaine of rheumes, catarhs and poses. Then had we none but reredosses, and our heads did never ake. For as the smoke in those daies was supposed to be a sufficient hardning for the timber of the house; so it was reputed a far better medicine to keepe the goodman and his familie from the quacke or pose, wherewith as then verie few were oft acquainted.*

With some changes to the spelling, the second paragraph of this quotation could as easily have been written in the present century!

The oak that was used was cut into beams, sometimes almost half a metre thick, using a two handed saw. The piece of timber to be worked was placed over a pit about two metres deep, and one sawyer stood on top of the work, holding one end of the saw, while the other unfortunate sawyer worked in the pit below.

As the frame was cut, it was assembled into its final shape, and all necessary adjustments made at the site of the sawpit. The carpenter then dismantled it, ensuring that each section was carefully marked to enable it to be reconstructed later on its final site. These joiner's marks, often in Roman numerals, can still be seen in the roof timbers of many of the old houses of the village.

The assembly of the frame was a major event in the village, with all the able-bodied men turning out to lend a hand. Once the frame was complete, the spaces between were filled with a lattice of interwoven twigs and branches known as wattle, and this was liberally plastered, or daubed, with mud.

Finally, the roof was covered either in thatch or in Horsham stone. This was produced by quarrying limestone or sandstone blocks, and leaving them standing on end through the winter, when water seeping into the porous stone would freeze and split the blocks into thinner roofing slabs.

The timber-frame method of construction produced a house which moved quite considerably as the timber settled and people moved around within the house. As a result, the wattle and daub infilling often left gaps, and so houses were sometimes further covered on the outside with wooden shingles to make them weatherproof. While these were short-lived, and none have survived, the concept is continued in the clay hanging tiles which are so common in the village.

Other changes were taking place at this time, both outside and inside the house. Returning to the chronicle of 1586:

> *There are old men yet dwelling in the village where I remaine, which have noted three things to be so marvellouslie altered in England within their sound remembrance...*
>
> *One is the multitude of chimnies latelie erected, whereas in their yoong daies there were not above two or three,... but eche one made his fire against a reredosse in the hall, where he dined and dressed his meat.*
>
> *The second is the great amendment of lodging, for our fathers have lien full oft upon straw pallets, on rough mats covered onlie with a sheet under coverlets made of dagswain or hopharlots, and a good round log under their heads in steed of a bolster or pillow. Pillows were thought meet onlie for women in childbed. As for servants, if they had anie sheet above them it was well, for seldome had they anie under their bodies, to keepe them from the pricking straws that ran oft through the canvas of the pallet, and rased their hardened hides.*
>
> *The third thing they tell of is the exchange of vessell, as of treene* (wooden) *platters into pewter, and wodden spoones into silver or tin.*

Banner House was built as a timber-framed house, and although the facade has been "improved", probably at the time of the second period of major structural change to the buildings of Tarring in the early nineteenth century, the underlying structure can still be seen on the north side of the house.

*8. Banner House, a shop until the 1960's, is now a private house. The original timber frame is exposed on the wall on the right.*

The building was originally a single dwelling, but was divided into two for a brief period between 1770 and 1793. In this period there was a brewhouse in the rear garden. After a further century as a single home, it was again divided, but in a different way, early in the present century.

The house has been much used as a shop in recent times, and as early as 1855 Charles Carter, a wheelwright, millwright and master baker was working here. By 1895 it was also a baker's shop, run by a Mrs Carter, probably the daughter of Charles, who worked and lived here until around 1920.

During this time, a local resident remembered walking from Heene Mill - which stood south of Mill Road in the vast Heene Field, on a site now occupied by numbers 33 to 37 Mill Road [20], and was demolished in 1903 - to buy bread at Mrs Carter's shop. The shop itself was on the north side of the door, and had a bow window. It sold

*9. Heene mill was demolished in 1903. This drawing was made in 1884, but the mill is shown on maps as early as 1587.*

sweets from glass jars by the pennyworth, and sherbet dabs at four for a penny, as well as groceries and freshly baked bread [21].

The High Street here was at its narrowest, and was of necessity two way. It was also a bus route before the opening of Rectory Road [22], and this must have caused considerable congestion at times. An occupant of Banner House at the time recalled watching the buses backing up when they met at this point.

Ron Brown, who took over the shop in 1921, extended it to the whole of the ground floor. He died on active service in the second war [23], and the shop was taken over by a grocery chain, but it remained in operation until well into the 1960's.

In 1650, the next group of houses, numbers 11 to 17, was the principal house of the tenement, a *capital* (in the sense of excellent) *messuage* with two barns and five acres of land paying rent of eight shillings and six pence and a cock each year. It was the home of Elizabeth Wheatley, the widow of John Wheatley, gentleman, and heir of Roger Kingston. The family were important landowners in seventeenth century Tarring.

John Hamper and his wife, later his widow, Margaret lived here

*10. High Street in 1933, when buses travelled along it in both directions.*

between 1669 and 1709, when John Cooper, and later his son William, moved in.

By 1750, there was also a building called a millhouse in the garden, but after this date the tenement was divided, and became a number of different homes. The barns behind became stables, and were later partly converted into a dwelling, sometimes as many as three separate homes. Stamford Rabson, a shopkeeper, was here in 1787, and William Holcombe, also a mercer and druggist in 1798. This suggests that the house was being used as a shop at this time.

The main house was also split up into smaller properties in about 1800, and by 1839 the building fronting the road had become four houses, as it was until recently, when numbers 11 and 13 were recombined. The Holcombe family continued to own at least part of the property until 1853. Number 11 was sometimes called Marion Cottage, and number 13 Hensons Cottage, probably after a shepherd named Henson who lived in the village, and possibly here, at the end of the last century.

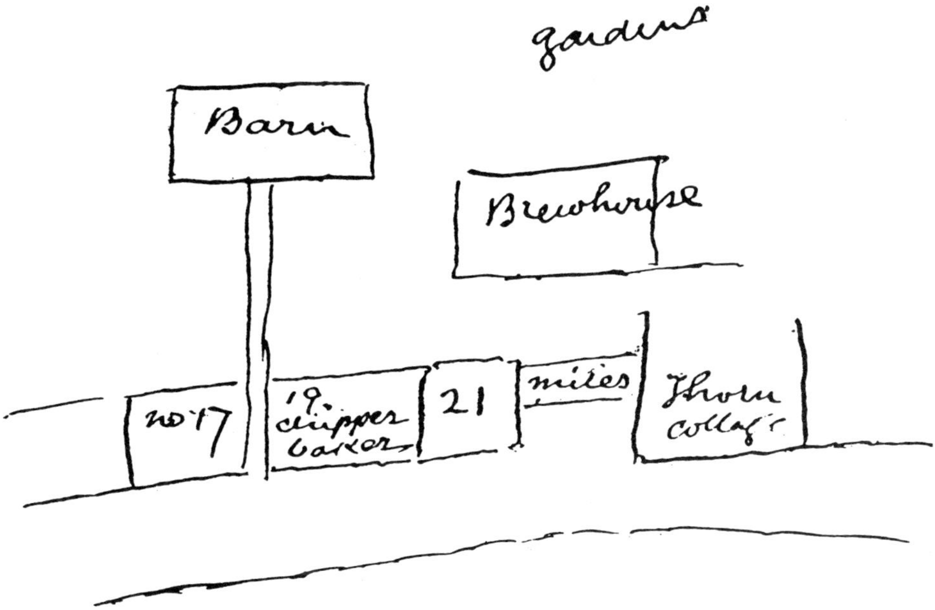


*11. The narrow path to the north of number 17 High Street led originally to a large barn known as the Millhouse. This sketch map, drawn in the 1920's, shows the approximate location of the barn, and of a brewhouse which once stood behind number 23.*

A fifth house, number 13a, survives behind this row, having been converted from a storeroom in the early nineteenth century. This little house is called Chippers, and the yard was known as Chippers Yard in 1861. It was the location of a substantial bootmaker's business run by Thomas Chipper and later Jesse his son.

The narrow passage which gives access to this cottage and the new bungalows recently built here, also originally provided access to the barns and houses which previously stood on this land. As a shared right of way, it seems to have caused regular problems in the past, with rights of passage sometimes being granted only for carts with a specific number of horses, and often only in the daytime.

The wall of number 17, to the south of this passage, has been rendered in modern times, but the rendering has broken away in places to reveal a wall of knapped flints. Although work like this is common in Sussex, it is quite unusual for Tarring.

*12. In knapped flintwork, each pebble is broken to reveal its smooth inner texture. The missing plasterwork on the north wall of 17 High Street reveals a section where the flints have also been carefully chosen to present faces of equal size, giving a very regular appearance.*

The two cottages on the north side of the entrance, numbers 19 and 19a, were always a separate house, but still a part of the extensive Wheatley tenement in 1650. There was a shop here in 1839, and the house, a single dwelling, was occupied by John Sayers, a cooper and farmer of 42 acres, providing employment for four men and a boy from the village. The front of number 19 still retains the appearance of the shop front, although it was entensively renovated a few years ago as a private house. In 1893 it was a baker's and grocer's shop run by yet another Chipper, this time Ambrose, and was sometimes called Wimborn House. The bakery must have been popular. It was regularly advertised in the parish magazine and elsewhere, and when H. B. Grice took it over in 1926, selling bread baked in an oven heated with wood, he was careful to include the name of the previous proprietor in the advertisement.

It is interesting to note the emphasis on the wood-burning oven. Gas and electricity (as alternative power sources) only arrived in the village at the end of the previous century, gas in 1881, and electricity some time after 1901, so it seems unlikely that an old-fashioned fuel would have had any consumer appeal over these new clean fuels. However, Luke, yet another Chipper, ran a coal merchant's business further up the street; perhaps there were problems with the quality of the coal, with smoke tainting the bread. Certainly the electricity generating plant was having problems, and was forced to use high quality, and costly, Welsh smokeless coal, with a consequent high price to the consumer. This led to the introduction in Worthing of one of the first diesel electric generators [24]. Nevertheless, domestic consumption of electricity at this time was very low. In 1911, the maximum demand for the whole of Worthing at any one time was 388 kilowatts, which represents approximately one sixty watt light bulb for each family in the town, or one half a bar of an electric fire for each house connected to the supply.

The shop has been a tobacconist's and a grocer's subsequently until the 1960's, when Mrs Emily Norris, who kept the shop then, retired.

The houses from number 21, northwards as far as the Vine, comprise a single tenement where Avicia Barnard died in 1647. The house that stood here then had been previously owned by at least two others, and so could not then have been very new.

In 1732, the owner, Walter Barton, borrowed fifty pounds for half a year at three per cent per annum on the security of the property, and when he died in 1739, the debt was still not repaid, although interest payments seem to have been made. In 1747, the matter was amicably resolved when Richard Fitzhenry, the heir of the lender, agreed to allow the tenement to be subdivided, and to accept half in repayment of the loan. This allowed Esther Barton, Walter's widow, to remain here, which she did until she died in 1766.

The division was done with some care, as the entry shows:

*All that dwelling house being part of the aforesaid messuage or tenement and the north end thereof containing twenty six foot in front with a Brewhouse behind it and a little Garden and all the north border to the West Stile and a passage up to the said Stile as likewise to an Orchard or piece of ground twenty three yards long from the said Stile Eastward and ten yards and an half wide from the said Stile Southward, the South side of the said piece of ground being twenty five yards long with a Stable or outlet standing therein, and the East side thereof thirteen yards and an half long and also to the use of the Well there with a passage through the entry at the South end or part of the other house into the Garden.*

In 1788, William Putteck divided the southern section again, and one house now had only a fifteen foot frontage. The northern section was owned by successive generations of the Russell family from 1765 to 1822. John Russell who lived here in 1798, was a postmaster [25], the first record of this profession in the village. It was to be sixty years before the penny post was introduced by Sir Rowland Hill, and letters, which were carried by coach or wagon, were relatively expensive to send. The Rector of Berwick, in his boyhood recollections of the early nineteenth century [26], wrote:

*No steel pens, so each person had to use quills and to know how to mend them. Blotting paper was in use, but sand was more generally used, and always kept in its proper place, in a thing like a pepper castor, in each inkstand. Wafers were used to fasten papers together, and every gentleman carried his own seal. Of course envelopes were unknown. There was no penny post, the postage of a letter from London to Lewes was eightpence, and if the smallest scrap of paper was put inside the folded sheet double postage was charged. Letters from a distant part of England often cost three or four shillings.*

*The letter was a sheet of paper, folded so as to leave a blank space for the direction, and fastened by being sealed down. Inside, the paper was often covered every square inch with writing crossed and sometimes recrossed. Letters were not prepaid, but the postman collected the postage on delivery.*

*Poor people could not afford to have letters, and so it was often years before they heard even of the death of a relative living at a distance.*

However, Sussex men were always inventive, and our writer continued:

*One common device to get to know if a friend or relation was still alive, was to get a sheet of paper, direct, seal and post it to the absent one. The person whose name was on the letter would know the writing, and refuse to take it in, saying he or she could not afford the postage. Then the person whose name was on the letter would get another blank sheet and direct it to the sender of the first sheet, who also would refuse to take in the letter. Other devices were to have pre-arranged signals; for instance, if a letter came addressed to Mrs W White, Mrs White would know that the sender was well - Mrs I White that the sender was ill - Mrs B White better, and so on.*

If these practices were well known to a vicar, it seems likely they were widespread, and they conjure up pictures of mail coaches, speeding their way up and down the country, heavily laden with blank sheets of paper being conveyed for no charge. No wonder the mail was so expensive!

This house was also subsequently divided again, and what had little more than one hundred years previously been a single tenement, became by 1839 four separate dwellings.

Number 21 was used by a furniture dealer between 1896 and 1902, and this house was at one time, appropriately enough, called Castle View. Number 23 was also sometimes a shop. It was the premises of a wireless engineer in the 1930's, and a wool shop after the war.

*13. The top photograph shows the Vine in the High Street at the turn of the century. The appalling state of the roadway can be clearly seen. The same scene today illustrates how little the street has changed.*

CHAPTER THREE

# THE VINE

Once again, this is an ancient holding, and a further tenement held by Avicia Barnard at the time of her death in 1647, when the property was described as being previously owned by Streeter. The facade of the building appears to belong to the nineteenth century. Although it looks at first sight to be constructed from stone blocks, this is almost certainly not so. The surface is probably cement rendering, using Portland cement, which was first discovered by the Romans. However, when they left Britain, the technique was lost, and only rediscovered in the late eighteenth century. The surface was often incised with a trowel when wet to give the impression of the joins of real stonework.

As originally built, the facade had three identical bays to the south of the passageway, each with a single door. Sometime in the present century, the two outer doors were replaced with windows, and the central bay removed on the ground floor to provide a more impressive entrance. This change is not apparent from an examination of the present building, and is only evidenced by an early photograph. This little feature is a good illustration of how much small and unrecorded change takes place in domestic buildings over the years. There is very likely a timber frame hidden beneath the present frontage, and the buildings in the garden at the back also appear old.

From the seventeenth to the nineteenth centuries, this tenement was called a messuage with barn, orchard and garden, and there are still apple trees in the garden. Each year, on January 5th, the Eve of Epiphany, the Sompting Village Morris visit the village. After dancing up and down the street, they repair to the Vine where they perform the old Sussex custom of howling or wassailing the apple trees in the garden. The ceremony involves dancing round the tree in a ring, while beating it with sticks. The custom is a relic of pagan worship of nature, and is meant to ensure a good harvest. An additional feature of the event in modern times is the consumption of copious quantities of beer! The dancers also visit the village on that other great pagan festival of May Day.

*14. Morris dancers visit the High Street regularly. Here, the Sompting Village Morris are celebrating May Day.*

In 1811, the property was occupied by Naves Phillips, who later took over the copyhold. He was a schoolmaster, and ran a school called the West Tarring Academy. In a contemporary book [27], the school is described as *an excellent and well regulated school, conducted upon the best principles, both as to the care of body and mind. The maternal conduct of Mrs Phillips towards the infants under her charge, reflects more credit on her than any thing that can be said by us in her favour.*

Despite this fulsome praise, the school appears to have been short lived. By 1828, Naves Phillips, although still the copyholder, is described as *County schoolmaster, now of Worthing.* Presumably the rapid growth of Worthing, following the emergence of the fashion for sea bathing, presented greater opportunities for his talents.

1843 saw the arrival of Richard Parsons. He started business as a beer retailer, and presumably also a brewer, and the Parsons family continued to brew and sell beer here until after 1936. The building was first referred to as the Vine brewery in 1894. Even as recently as 1953, the occupier was described in the Worthing directory as a beer retailer rather than a publican, and the Vine was not called a public house until about 1956. It is thus by far the newest pub in the village.

Brewing played an important part in village life before this century. Prior to the arrival of piped water and sewers in Tarring in the late ninteenth century,the purity of water was often a problem, since it was drawn from the numerous wells in the village, and sewage was frequently thrown into the street to await the next fall of rain. Drinking water was neither safe nor pleasant, so beer was used as a natural substitute and consumption was far higher than today. It is easy to romanticise over the style of life in times gone by, but the reality could not have been pleasant, particularly in hot dry weather. The conditions undoubtedly contributed to the spread of plague in the Middle Ages and to the serious outbreak of typhoid at the end of the nineteenth century.

The house at number 31 is obviously now a part of the Vine facade, and it was also a part of the earlier house. The site next on the north, now Croft Cottage, was a garden in 1875, but the present house had been constructed by 1898. For a short while in the period 1916 to 1920, these two cottages were called Brewery Cottages.

Northwards from here to the Becket on this side of the road, there are no physical remains of Tarring before 1800, all of the earlier houses having been demolished and replaced during the last two hundred years. Nevertheless, there are connections with earlier times in evidence in the names and positions of some of the more recent houses.

Next to the north, we arrive at a very typical Victorian terrace of five houses. The first reference to it was in the Worthing directory for 1904, and so in fact it was probably completed in the reign of Edward VII rather than Victoria. Its origins are certainly Victorian however, as it was originally called Princes Terrace, although this name was not in use by 1920. This seems to be a further little commentary on the times. In 1900, perhaps when the initial plans for the site were being prepared, Queen Victoria had been on the throne for 63 years. Her eldest son and heir Edward, Prince of Wales, was very much the man about town, and very popular among the populace. To identify the terrace with him would have seemed an excellent idea. However, just ten years later, not only had the Queen died, but Edward, then King Edward VII, had succumbed too, from an attack of bronchitis. Although he had five sons who bore the title Prince, they were all still children, and in those days, unlike today, were kept well away from public attention. All in all, the name Princes Terrace would have seemed not such a good idea, and was soon forgotten.

*15. Princes Terrace was built in about 1904. The original slate roof of number 37, the second house from the left, has been replaced with modern tiles since this photograph was taken.*

Here again we can see considerable evidence of the minor architectural changes that take place over the years. The original slate roofs have one by one been replaced with modern tiles, and replacement windows, new front doors, gates and painted brickwork are all in evidence. Despite these variations, the terrace retains its essential unity, and it would be nice to hope that one day it will revert to its original name of Princes Terrace.

Before the terrace was built, this land contained a strange jumble of buildings. On the site of number 35 was an old timber-framed house. It dated back at least to 1650, when it formed part of the estate of Elizabeth Wheatley, who, as we have seen, lived farther down the street.

Fronting the street on the site of numbers 41 and 43 was a large barn, which again dated back to the middle of the seventeenth century. At that time it belonged to the South family, who lived in a house near Tarring Recreation Ground. We will meet them again later in the walk. At the rear of the barn was a hogpen which originally belonged to Bolds, a tenement on the other side of the street.

At the beginning of the nineteenth century, John Barker, the first of a family of maltsters who lived at Highfield, progressively took over all of these properties, and in 1843 bought the freehold. A house was built on the garden in the south west corner of the site between 1875 and 1898, which today is number 45, and a further building stood to the north of this, at the end of the drive on the north side of the terrace. It was built between 1898 and 1913, and still stood in 1966, although it has since been demolished. Between 1926 and 1930 it was used as a school, run by Miss Mary Michell.

This is the second school we have discovered so far in the High Street, and we will eventually discover a third at the Old Palace. The earliest mention of a school in Tarring was in 1713, when twelve boys were said to be taught at the charge of the Rector of the Parish. Over the years, the standard of education seems to have been very variable. John Warter, who was Vicar of Tarring between 1834 and 1878, wrote [28]:

> *When I first came into this Parish there were no regularly established Parochial Schools, and the people generally were no scholars, - their own form of expression. Thirty years ago few wrote, and those who did, wrote imperfectly. The cross in attestation was the common signature.*

However, a Government survey of 1818 made the remarkable claim that hardly any adult in the parish was unable to read!

Immediately to the north of the gravel drive are two modern

garages. The house behind, Rose Cottage, is also very recent, dating from around 1970, although the name may have been inherited from number 45, which was also called Rose Cottage for a short while at the turn of the century.

A row of three old flint thatched cottages used to stand on the site of these garages, with their doors opening directly onto the road. The building dated back at least to 1668, when Henry Stiles took it over from George Hide, and in 1808, when James Burtenshaw took over the copyhold, the house had recently been divided into three, and presumably "modernised", as was usual at the time.

Whether or not the conversion was done with the care and quality of workmanship which has preserved other houses in Tarring for many hundreds of years, can be judged from the fact that by 1925, the building, then called Stents Cottages, was almost derelict, and had to be demolished. The Worthing Gazette wrote at the time [29]:

*Many will regret, for artistic as well as for sentimental reasons, that three of the old thatched cottages in Tarring High-street are about to disappear.... The cottages soon to be reduced to a heap of debris are not nearly so old as their better-known neighbours on the opposite side of the High-street, but they have withstood the wear and tear of more than a century, until now they are nothing more than a rapidly disintegrating mass of thatch, timber, flints, and plaster - a constant menace not only to those whom they have housed for years but to passers-by in the street.*

*Picturesqueness in architecture we all admire, and the cottage homes of our county are worthy of preservation wherever possible, but the most ardent lover of antiquity, passing along Tarring High-street one day, might be pardoned if, on finding three thatched cottages collapsing like a pack of cards about his ears, he was overheard to remark: 'Picturesqueness be blowed!'*

*16. A rare photograph of Stents Cottages, which were demolished in 1925. The wall enclosing the field called Obletts can be seen on the right. There has been so much change at this end of the High Street in the present century, that it is hard to believe the lower photograph shows the same scene today!*

*17. The rear of Stents Cottages. The wall on the left belongs to Magpie Cottage, number 53. It has subsequently been rendered, and the house extended to the south.*

The conversion of these three cottages was only part of a larger scheme. James Burtenshaw, a bricklayer, bought all the land from here north to include what is now number 57 from John Pelling, and divided the remaining land into three plots. The most northerly plot he sold to Jonathon Groves, another bricklayer, and the centre plot to William Hide, a carpenter. The third plot, on which stood an old barn, he kept for himself.

James was granted license on July 15th 1808 by the lord of the manor *to pull down the barn ... Upon Condition That the said James Burtenshaw do and shall within the space of twelve months from the date hereof ...build a Good and Substantial House on the said Premises in lieu of such Barn.*

Presumably the three worked as a sort of co-operative, and built the three houses which are now numbers 53, 55 and 57. They have had numerous owners and several names since their construction. Numbers 53 and 55 were often called Bay Cottages in the early twentieth century, and number 57, the home of the Duffields for many years, was known as Wisteria.

*18. Stents Cottages looking south, before they fell into disrepair, and the same scene today.*

*19. This line drawing, from about the same viewpoint as the previous photograph, shows the barn which stood to the south of Stents Cottages. The garden wall of the Hollies had not then been built, and another large barn stood on the site of the old barber's shop.*

Moving north again, number 61 is the site of yet another very old cottage which disappeared early in the present century. Since 1682, it had been part of a tenement which extended to both sides of the street. The premises opposite were used at various times as a malthouse, shops and a blacksmith, but the owner always lived in the little cottage on this side of the street.

At least four generations of the Hollands family, the village blacksmiths, lived here between 1821 and 1930, latterly running an ironmonger's shop here in addition to the garage on the other side of the street, but soon afterwards the old cottage was demolished and the present house built in its place.

The old peoples' home on the next site is very modern. Originally, the fields of Church Farm bordered directly onto the road here. The fields were called the Bartons, as they were closest to the farm buildings, which were on the site of Church Way - barton is an old English word for a farmyard. By 1880 the land was being used to grow

*20. These houses were built by James Burtenshaw in 1808, on the site of one of the many barns in the High Street.*

fruit, and over the next fifty years, a large area of glasshouses was built on the south of the site, where the garages at the end of Church Way now stand.

Tarring generally saw considerable development of the market gardening and fruit growing industry during this period, and it was not until after the Second World War that the fields and orchards which surrounded the High Street were gradually replaced with housing, and the village irrevocably lost its rural environment, becoming instead an island of history in the uniformity of modern suburban Worthing.

The growing of fruit and vegetables in Tarring dates back many hundreds of years, as witnessed by the parsonage fig gardens, but in the nineteenth century, it developed into an important local industry. In the years after 1850, the number of nurseries, and men employed in them, grew rapidly, and the industry received a considerable boost with the arrival of the railway in Worthing in 1845. Distribution was further improved with the opening of West Worthing station, and the construction of the Cliftonville curve at Brighton in 1879, which allowed through trains to run to London for the first time.

Worthing was the home of the pioneers of the glasshouse crop industry, and the first commercial greenhouses in the world were built in Broadwater in 1870, reportedly using glass purchased from the Great Exhibition in Hyde Park in 1851. Hothouse tomatoes were also first cultivated in Worthing, and it was the experience of the early growers here that led to the development of the industry in the Channel Islands, Belgium and the Netherlands, as apprentices were sent from these countries to the local nurseries.

When they were first introduced, tomatoes were large and irregular in shape, and it took many years for them to become truly popular. Their cause could not have been improved in their early years by the fact that they were known as love apples, a rather unappealing name, in spite of the implication of aphrodisiac properties.

By 1905, a special goods station had been built at West Worthing to distribute the widely praised crops of early glasshouse fruits and vegetables of the district. Initially, the principal product of the growers was grapes, which were later joined by tomatoes, cucumbers and exotic fruits. The First World War saw tomatoes emerge as the principal crop, as they gradually gained in popularity amongst an initially sceptical public.

Later, mushroom growing developed, and there are still mushroom farms in the area. This is somewhat ironic, since the nursery trade was originally encouraged by the temperate climate of Sunny Worthing, from which mushrooms have to be shielded!

CHAPTER FOUR

# THE BECKET

Fairoak Court is another example of relatively modern buildings on a site with a long history. In 1610, this area was part of an estate called Emeries. It was a yardland or virgate; a measure of land used in the Domesday book, and extended to some thirteen and a half acres. By 1669 a house and a barn had been built here, and in 1730, Edmund Sayres, a maltster, took possession. This was the start of an association between the property and the Sayers family which was to last almost two hundred years.

Living here, Edmund would have experienced the earthquake [30] which hit Tarring on the morning of 25th October, 1734. It lasted only for a few seconds, but was also felt in Shoreham, Chichester and Havant, and worse near the coast. As far as can be ascertained, there was no structural damage or personal injury, but there were a number of stories of drawers rattling and pictures falling off walls.

The more detailed descriptions came from residents of Chichester, but the shock was less strong there than at Tarring. John Freeland, a maltster from Chichester, said that *as he lay in his bed he all on a sudden heard a great cracking of the stairs and at the same time found the whole frame of his bed as it were to move, at which he was very greatly surprized and very believes it to have been the shock of an Earthquake.*

John Lang, a Chichester alderman, gave an even more graphic account. He reported that *as he lay in Bed wide awake on Friday morning last being the 25th of October inst between the hours of three and four in the morning and nearer four than three to the best of his knowledge He all of a sudden felt as it were the whole bed under him to move and as he afterwards lay thinking of this so sudden motion he questioned with himself whether some great dog was not under the bed, and when he got up in the morning (himself being very fat and unwieldy) ordered his servant to look under the bed, and nothing being found he immediately thought twas the shock of an earthquake, and when he went abroad he heard it much talk't of by people of the city who all agreed as to the time of this accident.*

On Edmund's death in 1756, the house was taken over by his youngest brother John, and a succession of John Sayers, fathers and sons, lived and worked from here. They also owned the malthouse next to the George and Dragon, continuing the family business as maltsters and corn merchants there, although they still lived here.

John Lindup Sayers, who was born in 1838, occupied the house from 1884 until he died in the 1930's. He recorded [31] that it was an old farmhouse with a cellar, together with a barn and farm buildings which were used for a time as a brewery for the Vine. The house was called Fairoak for the first time in 1905, but by 1946 it had been demolished. The present development, which was built soon afterwards, commemorates the old house in its name, Fairoak Court.

Up until 1905, this was the last house in the village on this side of the road. Subsequently, much development took place to the north, and five houses were built in the next few years. Highdown Avenue was constructed by 1914, and Becket Buildings, with its impressive mock tudor facade, had been completed by 1930. Subsequently, the road frontage has been completely developed, and some of the original houses have been replaced by more modern buildings.

A little way to the west on the north side of the Littlehampton Road, what is now called Durrington Recreation Ground was once a field belonging to the chantry of St Mary in Tarring church. The chantry provided an income independent of the vicarage and rectory, and existed from before 1282 until the sixteenth century. The field was known as Chantry Field, and the barn that stood on it until about 1930, Chantry Barn.

The original path from Tarring to Salvington crossed the Littlehampton Road here, and was called Chantry Lane. As late as the beginning of this century, it was still a leafy country lane, and its name is commemorated in Chantry Road nearby, which, with the surrounding streets, was built soon afterwards.

*21. Fairoak Farmhouse, home of the Sayers family for many years, and Fairoak Court, which replaced it after the war.*

*22. Becket Buildings, seen, above, soon after it was built in 1930, looks much the same today. The lower photograph shows the view along Poulters Lane before the building to the north of the junction had been constructed.*

23. *The Littlehampton Road in 1906, looking west from the Yeoman.*

Before the turn of the present century, the road north through Tarring was called High Street until it reached the Arundel Road at Offington Corner. It crossed the road from Broadwater to Goring at what is now sometimes known as Poulters Corner. This crossroads goes back at least five hundred years, being mentioned as Polltree in 1418. Subsequently the fields to the south were often referred to as Poultry Fields, but it is unlikely that the name originated from any association with chickens. More probably it refers to a tree which has had its top cut off, known as a polled tree. The Arundel Road from Chichester to Brighton is older still, and largely follows the course of a road built by the Romans [32].

Tarring High Street led north from Fairoak to Horsham by way of Findon, and the continuous line of the original road is apparent. It could not have been in good condition, because although it is mentioned in the fifteenth and sixteenth centuries, the carters preferred to use the alternative but very steep road over the Downs to Steyning [33] in 1798. In this, the road had much in common with many of the other roads of Sussex, which were notorious for their bad state of repair, particularly in winter when they were often quite impassable. Indeed, it was traditionally said that a horse could drown in the mud on many a Sussex road before the Turnpike Acts of the late eighteenth century began at last to provide the necessary funds to finance their improvement.

The road gave access to the hamlet of Marlpost, just south of Horsham, near Christ's Hospital. At least 40 acres of land here belonged to the manor of Tarring, often in fact called Tarring with Marlpost, since 1282, and probably from much earlier. The Domesday book listing of a woodland for six swine in Tarring may well be a reference to Marlpost. It was quite common for the manors of the Sussex coastal plain to own land in the Weald, as it gave them access to the considerable amounts of wood that grew there. In the thirteenth century, one of the services that copyhold tenants were required to perform for the lord of the manor was the carrying of one cartload of wood from Marlpost each year for every virgate of land held. This was a not inconsiderable task, given the state of the road, and carrying two and a half cartloads was reckoned as a week's work for one man.

There were also copyhold tenants living at Marlpost, and they were entitled to graze their pigs and other animals in common in the woods. Similar rights still exist today in the New Forest. The land at Marlpost was eventually sold by the manor to the Duke of Norfolk in 1806.

The most northerly site with a long history on the east side of the street is Highfield, one of a group of houses set well back from the road, at the end of a drive beginning about half way between Broomfield Avenue and the Thomas a'Becket Middle School entrance. The Thomas a'Becket Hotel was built around 1910, and the other houses on this side of Rectory Road were built in piecemeal fashion between about 1930 and the present day. The block immediately south of the hotel is about fifty years old, and is called Canterbury Buildings.

The site of Highfield itself, now number 104, was a field called Northfield in 1688, which by 1722 had appurtenances, or minor properties, associated with it. These were probably farm buildings, though almost certainly not a dwelling house. A messuage and other buildings did, however, stand on the land by 1793. In 1843, the site formed part of the extensive estate to which John Barker bought the freehold, and a malthouse had been built here. The present house had

*24. Highfields is now a private house, set well back from Rectory Road. It was originally called Highfield, and was the home of the Barker family for many years. The watercolour by E. Martin, top, shows archery practice in the grounds in 1850.*

been built by 1850, and at the end of the century, the property, known as Highfield Farm, was one of the most important farms in the area, run by Edwin Lephard. He installed gas lighting to the house [34], which was still in use in 1956.

In a letter to the Worthing Herald in 1956, John Holland, a member of the family of Tarring blacksmiths, wrote [35]:

> *I have known Highfield since before Mr Edwin Lephard went there. Mr John Barker lived there and was a farmer and maltster. I remember him being pushed about in a bathchair by his old maltster Mr Streeter. Mr Barker died in 1880 and is buried in Tarring churchyard. According to a ledger of my grandfather's, dated 1803, he did smithing work for a Mr Barker at this date and onwards. This Mr Barker must have been the father of John. He died in 1860 and is also buried in Tarring churchyard. So Highfield was there before 1808. I myself have done smithing work for Mr Edwin Lephard and Mr Percy Lephard, who had one of the finest teams of cows in Sussex, and was also one of the best farmers.*

As we cross Rectory Road to return to High Street, we also arrive back in the area of Tarring where houses have stood for at least 300 years. The first small terrace of three cottages, numbers 66 to 70, was probably built in around 1865 by William Kennard, a carpenter and builder who lived here for many years with his daughter, who ran a day school in Tarring. They have been considerably altered in recent years. Before their construction, the land had been occupied by a little cottage, owned by Clement Quimby in 1630.

The three cottages were originally called Alpha, Omega and Tabeal Cottages, and some of these names survived until relatively recently. Joseph Honey lived here in 1913, and still in 1975.

The new development numbered 44 to 64a and Dorset Place, won an architectural award when it was constructed in the late 1970's. The site was originally three mediaeval tenenements, and the ownership of all three can be traced back to the seventeenth century. The land now occupied by 64 and 64a was described in 1654 as *a cottage with a small barn and about a rood of land called Keypins at the upper end of the towne of Tarringe.* It payed rent to the manor of 4d per annum, and was recorded as previously owned by Peeters, a name associated with at least two other sites in the village.

Peter Chipper took occupation in 1654. Jervius Chipper, who lived in Tarring in 1630, could well have been Peter's father, but there were no Chippers in Tarring in 1610. There are no earlier references yet found to this old Tarring name, which is still reflected in a number of places in the area, including Chippers Cottage at number 22 High Street and Chippers Road near Castle Road. In 1841 the census recorded no less than eight separate families of this name, with a total of 29 children. They do not appear to have prospered financially, however, as all but one of the breadwinners was working as an agricultural labourer. In 1903 the Worthing directory still listed six Chipper families in the village, but they have declined in the present century. By 1974, there were only four in West Tarring, and though the 1988 telephone directory lists seven names in Worthing, none live in the village.

Returning to our cottage: by 1671 it was being used as a smith's forge, one of four such sites in the High Street, and it remained so for over a hundred years until 1786. John Bennett, who was admitted to the tenancy in that year, was a surgeon. He is unlikely to have occupied it as a smithy, but there is no record of him seeking the necessary permission from the lord to let the property. By 1839 it was described as a house, shop and garden. The building was subsequently divided into two cottages, and was later demolished.

The second tenement covered the site of Dorset Place and numbers 60 and 62. In 1671 it consisted of a malthouse with an orchard and garden. It was occupied by the tenant of the cottage opposite, now number 61, and this remained so until the present century. In 1821 Edward Hollands, a blacksmith, was admitted, and in 1839 the property comprised shops with a garden. In 1856 Edward died, and left the tenancy to his son Thomas, also a blacksmith.

By this time, the property was described as a blacksmith's shop, formerly a malthouse, with barn, stables, orchard and garden, previously owned by, among others, Selden. It seems likely that sometime after 1786, the smithy moved a few yards down the street to the malthouse, which would have been larger, perhaps to reflect additional business produced by the then rapidly growing town.

Thomas Hollands was listed as blacksmith for the last time in 1887 and subsequently only Mrs Hollands' name appears. Mr Haffenden took over the business, and expanded it to serve the growing sophistication of life in the village. In 1898 his advertisement in the directory described the business as *J Haffenden, Shoeing, jobbing and general Smith. Gas, cold and hot water engineer, and agent for lawn mowers.* It seems that the property remained in the Hollands family, however, and in 1902 it had become John Hollands, blacksmith.

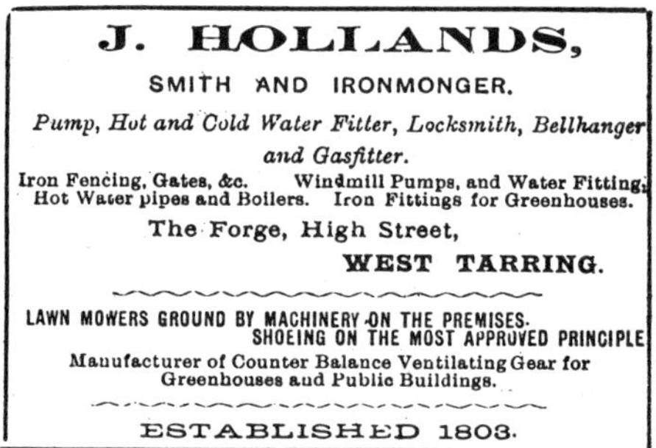

*25. These two advertisements, from the parish magazine in 1909 and 1910, show the transition of John Hollands' forge in the High Street from a smithy to a motor garage.*

Certainly the Hollands' business continued to prosper, and adapted to the increasing pace of change. In 1910, for the first time it was advertised not as just as a blacksmith but as *J Hollands - Engineer, smith and ironmonger, motor and cycle agent.* With the growing popularity of the motor car, the smithy eventually became Hollands Garage by 1921. It survived the loss of land in the rear for the construction of Rectory Road in the 1930's, and is still remembered by some of the longer-standing inhabitants of the village.

A pair of semi-detached cottages had been built on the north end of this site at around the turn of the century. They fell derelict in the 1940's and were demolished in 1956 to allow further extension of the garage, which by this time occupied the site of Dorset Place, too, with access both to High Street and to Rectory Road. As Auto Bodies Repair Company, it finally made way for the present development, incorporating the new garage in Rectory Road, in the late 1970's.

The remaining tenement, the site of numbers 44 to 58, was always an enclosed meadow called Obletts. In 1610 it was owned by John Selden, another name closely associated with Tarring. Although the name is well known locally, the man is less so, except by students of English history. In fact, John Selden played a part in the upheavals which led to the Civil War, and the execution of King Charles I.

Born in Salvington in 1584, Selden studied law at Oxford, and practised as a lawyer. He wrote a number of books, including a history of England, but he first came to prominence in 1617, when he published an essay which questioned the moral right of the Church to levy tithes. This challenge to the authority of the most powerful influence in the land after the Crown did not go unnoticed, and he was summoned to account for himself to the Privy Council. He avoided having to recant his views, being required only to express his regret that they had been published. In 1623, he entered Parliament, and by this time he was also a nationally known lawyer of considerable standing.

In 1629, the struggle for power between the King and Parliament was reaching crisis point, and following a violent scene in Parliament, Selden was arrested on the orders of the King and imprisoned in the Tower of London. He was eventually released in 1631 and went on to publish a number of books on the history of law and the rights of man. His determination to challenge accepted thinking with acute insight continued to lead him into difficulties until the revolution of 1642.

Subsequently his ideas were more widely acceptable, and in 1647, he was awarded £5000 damages for what was by then regarded as his unlawful imprisonment. He was a notable scholar of the Orient, and his extensive library on this and other subjects is preserved at the Bodleian Library in Oxford. Selden died in 1654 and was buried with considerable pomp in the Temple Church in London.

Obletts was owned in 1806 by William Margesson, a gentleman who lived in Offington Place, and remained a meadow surrounded by a flint wall until the new development began. Some local residents can remember it being used to graze sheep. Obletts measured about one and a half acres. It owed rent to the lord of the manor of 6d in 1668, and this remained so until 1843 when Thomas Penfold bought the freehold. This works out at 4d an acre, a rate which occurs regularly in the court rolls. In fact, it dates back to 1381.

In that year Wat Tyler led a revolt of peasants with the objective of hastening the replacement of villein services by money rents. The rebels, having established themselves in London and beheaded the Archbishop of Canterbury, were met by the young King Richard II, who granted them commutation of all servile dues in return for a rent of 4d an acre. Subsequently, Wat Tyler was killed on the orders of the Mayor of London, and the Government put down the rebellion and rescinded their agreement. Nevertheless, the standard of rent at 4d an acre was to survive for five hundred years.

CHAPTER FIVE

# THE HOLLIES

The Hollies is the first seriously old house remaining on this side of the street, but from here on southwards, almost every building has a long history. The neat flint facade dates from 1774, when this was one of the first of many houses in the village to be "modernised", but its origins go back to the reign of Queen Elizabeth I. Within the present fabric, traces of the original timber-framed building can be found, and evidence of the former projecting upper storey can be seen in the thickness of the walls.

John Evans, Vicar of Tarring from 1601 to 1605, came from Wales, and owned a house here. By 1610, the house was occupied by Eleanor Evans, John's widow, and was described as a mansion house, with a barn and garden. This was, however, the original use of the word mansion, as a place where someone lived, rather than the more modern meaning of a grand house.

There was considerably more land attached to the house than at present, extending back to the far side of what is now Rectory Road, although this was still a very modest plot by the standards of the time. It was a reflection, perhaps, of the fact that the occupant was sufficiently well off not to have to provide for himself and his family by growing, on his own land, most of what they ate.

In 1641, James Evans, John's grandson, inherited the house and immediately sold it to Thomas Botting, who was accumulating a substantial estate of houses, shops and land in the village [36]. Besides this house, where he lived with his wife Elizabeth, he owned six further houses, and all the eight shops that were described as such in the court rolls, although there were almost certainly others. He also owned over 40 acres of land in this manor alone, and a windmill at Salvington.

The house at this time was already substantial, befitting a man of property, and in 1662 admitted to four hearths, one of the largest numbers in the village. On the death of Elizabeth as a widow in 1663, the house passed from her son Stephen through a number of owners until it was bought by Richard Hedgecock in 1774.

He had grand plans for the house, and immediately set about a substantial rebuilding. Inspection shows the evident care that was lavished on the facade, and then, as now, it must have attracted admiring looks from passers-by. This attention to detail gave way to a rougher practicality, however, at the sides and rear of the building. The evidence is still there to see on the north wall, although the south elevation has been rendered in modern times.

*26. The Hollies as it looks today. Apart from the low wall in front, which dates from the present century, and the gates to the drive, it would have looked much the same immediately after its reconstruction in 1774.*

The flints in the facade of this house, as in almost all the flint walls in the village, are set in lime mortar. This was made by burning limestone in a furnace to make quicklime, then wetting or slaking it to produce slaked lime. This was mixed with sand and water to make the mortar that was used until the introduction of Portland cement in the nineteenth century.

Modern brick buildings generally rely on cavity walls and damp proof courses to prevent moisture penetrating the fabric, whereas older buildings were designed to allow moisture absorbed by the walls to evaporate to the outside. Lime mortar is much more porous than cement, and this was an important factor in assisting the evaporation. The house was kept dry inside simply by using walls thick enough to ensure that moisture evaporated from the outside before it was able to penetrate the full thickness of the wall.

The necessary limestone was dug from the side of the Downs at a chalk pit which can still be seen at the end of Foxley Lane. The need for suitable limestone was so important to the local economy that the right of Tarring residents to take chalk from here was specially mentioned and preserved in the tithe apportionment of 1839. In fact, it appears that we are still entitled to take chalk without limit, which may cause some consternation to the owners of the houses which now stand on the top edge of this quarry!

The house at this time was only some five metres from front to back, the depth of the original timber frame, and the Hedgecocks, Richard and Mariah, proudly proclaimed their contribution to the modernisation of Tarring by inserting an ornamental brick in what was then the rear wall, inscribed with their initials and the date.

*27. The date brick in The Hollies, commemorating the renovation of the house by Richard and Mariah Hedgecock in 1774. Originally on the outside back wall of the house, it is now on an interior wall.*

The rebuilding was not without cost however, and the next year, Richard took out a mortgage on the house from John Oliver for £160 at 4%, and finally, in 1778, sold the house to him. Oliver was another character from the history of the area, better known perhaps as the Miller of Highdown.

Highdown Mill stood at the summit of Highdown Hill, and the miller lived in a cottage nearby, on the edge of the woods to the north of the hill. Highdown House itself is of much later construction, dating from the early nineteenth century. The mill still survived [37] in 1805, but was apparently demolished [38] in 1826. The site can just be discerned as a circle of rough waste ground at the south west corner of the earthworks, due south of the triangulation point. The depression in the middle marks the site of the post in the centre of the mill. To the north, can be seen the remains of the pits used to dispose of the rubbish the milling process generated. It is interesting to see that over a century after the disappearance of the mill, the site is still very clearly distinguishable from the surrounding land, with nettles and other weeds thriving, and shows little sign of ever returning to downland grass.

John Oliver was an eccentric character, and busied himself in his spare moments constructing elaborate mechanical models. One of these, attached to the roof of his house during his lifetime, used wind power to operate a model of an exciseman chasing a smuggler, with an old woman at the officer's heels, laying about him with her broom. The theme of this creation has given rise to speculation that the miller, if not actually involved in smuggling, was at least sympathetic towards what was, at the time, one of the most widespread occupations in the area.

The greatest of the miller's eccentricities was reflected in his attitude to death. He constructed his own coffin, and kept it beneath his bed, with castors and a device for pulling it out rapidly if needed. He also built his own tomb, some twenty seven years before it was finally required. The tomb still stands on the hill, but recently was the subject of a particularly mindless attack when it was almost destroyed by a vandal with an earthmoving machine. Although it has been restored with considerable care, it now lacks the presence of the original structure, and some of the inscriptions have been lost. They were all recorded, however, by John Evans in his 1805 guide to Worthing, and are reproduced in appendix 5.

The funeral itself, when at last the time arrived, was a spectacular affair. Thousands of people attended from various and distant parts of the country. The corpse was carried from his house to the tomb by pall bearers dressed in white, and Ann Street of Goring, a young girl of twelve, also dressed in white, read a sermon of the miller's choosing.

To return to The Hollies, there was clearly some family connection between the Hedgecocks and John Oliver. Although the house had been sold to the miller in 1778, Mariah Hedgecock continued to live here, and on the miller's death in 1793, it was inherited by Mariah's eighteen year old son John Oliver Hedgecock. Indeed, it is possible that Mariah was the miller's daughter.

Thomas Burtenshaw bought the house in 1807, and after his death in the following year, it was inhabited by Rachael, his widow, until her death in 1823. This long period of widowhood must have made considerable inroads into any money left by her husband, and in her will [39], her effects were valued at less than one hundred pounds. The will itself provides an interesting commentary on the times:

*This is the last will and testament of me Rachael Burtenshaw of West Tarring in the county of Sussex widow made in an ill state of health but of sound disposing mind memory and understanding, whereby I mean to dispose of my worldly estate as follows, that is to say, I give and bequeath All my Copyhold Messuage or Dwellinghouse Yard Gardens and Premises situate in West Tarring aforesaid and within and holden of the Manor of Tarring with Marlpost unto my brother Edward Smith his heirs and assigns for ever subject nevertheless and I do hereby charge the same with the payment of all my just debts and funeral and testamentary expenses. I give and bequeath unto my said brother Edward Smith one set of china, ten wine glasses, one Kidderminster carpet, three Japan trays, a tea caddy, a tea kettle, one damask table cloth, one kitchen range and a fender, and I give and bequeath unto my niece Elizabeth Trevet twelve pounds and ten shillings to be paid out of my personal estate to buy her mourning and I likewise give and bequeath unto my said niece such further sum of money to be paid out of my personal estate as may be necessary to pay her small bills for clothes and medicines that she may have had at different times since her residing with me. I also give and bequeath unto my said niece my following wearing apparel viz two changes, one flannel petticoat, one camblett petticoat, one black silk gown,two lace caps, one white bonnett, one blue cloak, one yellow shawl, one night gown, and two night caps.*

The residue of her estate was left to the wife and daughters of her brother, and her good friend William Holcombe was appointed executor. The will was dated June 26th 1821, and following her death very soon afterwards, probate was granted on July 18th.

Richard Street bought the house in 1827, and the Misses Elizabeth and Letsy Street lived here for most of the remainder of the century. During this time, the orchard was sold to Mary Barker, who owned the Tribe estate next door. By 1890 the Misses Street had presumably both died, and the house was called The Hollies for the first time. In the 1920's Major General Robert Vaughan CB lived here after his retirement as Colonel Commandant of the Indian Army Service Corps. He was succeeded by Mrs Hylton, affectionately known as Lady Hylton, who lived here after the death of her husband, and died in the house as a recluse in 1979. The bootscrapers on either side of the door are modern replacements, but their presence indicates the state of the street in earlier days.

The next tenement extended from The Hollies south to the footpath, and back to the other side of Rectory Road. In 1647, Thomas Peeter and his wife Anne lived in a house here which was also used as a smith's shop. Forge and Becket Cottages are as old as this, and are probably the same building. By 1698, the estate had come into the hands of the Tribe family, who were to remain in continuous occupation until the second half of the nineteenth century.

Successive generations of owners were always called William Tribe, which is not as usual as you might first imagine, when you remember that property was inherited by the youngest son. One such William Tribe, in the early 1800's, built a much more impressive family home in the field behind the smithy, which was known later as Magnolia Cottage.

Mary Tribe, the last of the family to live here, was certainly doing so in some style in 1851 at the age of 82 years [40]. She employed 8 men and 2 boys to farm her 53 acres of land in the fields around her house, known originally as the Town Field, but later as Broadwater Field, and lived with her two unmarried daughters, a cook, a housemaid, and two nurses.

*28. This building, now known as Becket and Forge Cottages, is at least 350 years old. It was occupied for many years by the Tribe family, and converted into labourers' cottages when Magnolia Cottage was built in the early ninteenth century.*

She died soon afterwards, and the house passed through a number of hands over the next few years. When Glebe Road was originally built in 1893, it turned northwards at its eastern end, and provided an imposing access to this house, which was accordingly renamed Glebe House.

It was eventually demolished in 1933, as it stood directly in the path of the new Rectory Road [41]. The name Magnolia survived through Magnolia Nurseries, which for a time stood on the site of Orchard Avenue, but this too, finally gave way to the inexorable spread of suburban Worthing.

By 1839, the two cottages fronting the High Street were being used as homes for agricultural workers, and the site behind was a blacksmith's workshop. In 1894, William Lucas ran his wheelwright and coachbuilding business from here, and the rear wall of the old

*29. Glebe House, originally Magnolia Cottage, shortly before it was demolished in 1933 to make way for Rectory Road.*

barn in which he worked can still be seen as the back wall of the car park.

The small building at the entrance to the car park was built by George Fenner just before the First World War, when he sold his much larger grocer's shop in the market-place. It became a barber's shop in about 1950, run by Bill Berry. As such, it was very well supported by the local community, with queues often forming before opening time in the morning. Perhaps this had some connection with the fact that Bill never felt the need to increase his prices in line with inflation, or even at all. As a result, when he retired in 1988, it was still possible to get a good haircut here for 55p, or 50p for pensioners and children, compared to a minimum of around £2 anywhere else in Worthing at the time.

He was a versatile barber, and could often be seen through his open door coping efficiently with the most exotic hairstyles that modern youth could dream up. He was well acquainted with the neighbourhood, and could always be relied on to come up with another story of old Tarring. There were plans to develop the shop as an estate management office, but at the time of writing little progress has been made.

The premises behind slowly developed during the present century, becoming first the Tarring Motor and Engineering Company, then the Dominion Joinery Works. As the business grew, latterly in the ownership of Broad the builder, so the complaints from residents grew too, showing increasing concern over the noise of lorries and machinery, and the clouds of sawdust regularly thrown up and around the street by the wind. Eventually, in 1957, the town council stepped in, bought up the premises, and offered the company alternative accomodation in Northbrook Road, an offer that was accepted to the great relief of all around [42].

Subsequently, the old barn was demolished, and a plan was prepared to pedestrianize High Street south from this point, using the site as a turning circle for the northern end of the street, which was to become a cul-de-sac. The plan was never implemented, however, probably because of the difficulty in providing vehicular access to the rear of the houses on either side of the street to the south.

An alternative proposal, making the street one-way and access-only [43], was adopted in 1972, but no effective way has yet been found to enforce the access-only provision. The site of the old barn is still owned by the council, and is leased to the Vine as a car park.

The site of the houses presently numbered 30 and 32 is a mediaeval tenement called Bolds. A cottage with this name was recorded here in 1610, owned by Edward Weston. Tax was paid in respect of one hearth for it in 1662, which suggests it was a modest building, but this is by no means certain. The tax was universally disliked, and evasion was commonplace. There are many recorded instances of householders being caught out with undeclared fireplaces.

In 1650, when Jacob South and his wife Elizabeth inherited the property on the death of Richard White, it was described as *a messuage called Bolds, with a barn, an orchard and a garden containing about a rood, once Westons situated in the towne of Tarringe near the opening called the townfield gate.*

The footpath to the north would have been considerably wider in those days, as it constituted one of the entrances for farm carts from the High Street to the fields immediately behind the village. It was also the start of the footpath to Broadwater which followed the line of Wiston Road. The house also owned land on the other side of the

*30. A traditional Sussex game of stoolball being played on the Town Field. This watercolour, by E. Martin, was painted in 1856, looking west towards the church from what is now the junction of Glebe Road with Rectory Road.*

street, and this had been developed by 1721, when it included stables, and a barn which contained *certain edifices called a hogpen and hogsty.* These were sometimes separately owned and came with a right of way through the gates into the barnyard from the street.

Many of the inhabitants of Tarring would have kept pigs in those times, and even at the turn of the present century people could recall pigs being allowed to roam village streets in Sussex. In 1821, William Cobbett [44], commented on one of his rides through Sussex, *I saw, and with a great delight, a pig at almost every labourer's house.*

They would most likely have been the black and white Sussex pigs, descended originally from the wild boars of the forests of the lands of the South Saxons, from whom the name Sussex derives. Both the Saxons and the Normans regarded pork as the best eating meat, and it was the traditional Christmas dish in Sussex until very recently [45].

The keeping of pigs was a natural form of food storage before the days of refrigeration, and any family killing a pig would share the meat with their neighbours, expecting the gift to be returned in due course.

James Carter took over this property in 1775. His was an appropriate name, since he was in business as a carrier. He died in 1784, but his wife Mary carried on the trade.

The Universal British Directory [46], published in 1798, was a sort of primitive guide book to the towns of England at the time. Mary Carter, carrier, is listed among the principal traders, and the entry goes on to say:

*Carter's wagon sets out Monday and Wednesday, through Steyning, to the Queen's Head, Southwark; returns Friday evening in the summer, and Saturday morning in the winter.*

The fact that the wagon set out twice a week and apparently returned only once, shows that much care needs to be taken in relying on these old records!

The regular wagon run between London and Tarring carried not only goods but also people, although the journey was extremely arduous. Even the stage coaches in 1798 were badly sprung vehicles with wide iron wheels to cope with often apalling road conditions, but the wagon journey, with no springs at all, and like as not horses in poor condition, would only have been attempted out of grave necessity.

The wagoners route [47] took the traveller through Broadwater to Sompting and from there over the Downs to Steyning. In winter this section of the trip, over wet and slippery chalk, must have been the worst. The wagon took this road because it was one of only three roads north from Tarring at this time. The others, the roads over Salvington Hill to Storrington, and surprisingly, the road through Findon to Washington, were in even worse condition and often impassable except on horseback. The new road from West Grinstead to Worthing, now the A24, which eventually replaced the former muddy track, was only opened in 1804 following an Act of Parliament in 1802, to cater for the growing number of visitors attracted to Worthing.

Having negotiated the Downs, our wagon would now have found the journey considerably improved. The road from Steyning to

Horsham was considered to be one of the finest stretches of turnpike road in the country [48]. It is still a picturesque road, following the B2135 from Steyning through Ashurst and Partridge Green to join the A24 dual carriageway just south of Buck Barn crossroads. Many of the roads in the country at this time, including all of the Steyning to London road, were turnpikes. These were toll roads, with gates across at frequent intervals. The right to collect tolls was auctioned to the highest bidder, and the proceeds were used to maintain the roads. There were, in fact, twelve gates on the road between London and Tarring, so the journey must have been very much a stop-go affair.

It seems likely that the Carters' business did not continue much into the nineteenth century, with increasing competition from the growing Worthing trade, and it would certainly not have survived the coming of the railway to Shoreham in 1840 and to Worthing in 1845.

*31. This building, now over three hundred years old, was the house of the owner of the tenement called Bolds. In the nineteenth century it was subdivided, and later became known as Agnes Cottages.*

William Hide took possession of Bolds in 1808, and by 1825 had built a new cottage on part of the gates. The site of this is uncertain, but it could possibly be the northern section of the present building. Certainly the roof line suggests that the present house was not all built at the same time. A further building was shown to the north of this on the 1912 Ordinance Survey map.

By 1861 the main house had been divided into three cottages, and one was occupied by John Duffield, a blacksmith. Luke Chipper, who had lived in the village for some years, certainly lived in one of these cottages in 1895, and was described in the Worthing directory of that date as a coal merchant and fly proprietor, a fly being a small fast horse-drawn carriage, normally for hire. Perhaps he could have been carrying on the Carter business in a more modern form.

In 1900, the cottages were called Agnes Cottages for the first time, with number four to the south, and Luke Chipper at number three. In the Kelly's directory of 1951 there were still four separate occupants. However, in 1957, the Managing Director of the Tarring Joinery Works wrote a letter responding to complaints of noise and dust [49]. In it he said:

> *When we moved here in 1946, on the south side of us we had four cottages occupied by two very old people and two young working-class families and we never received complaints from them.... These four cottages were converted into two dwellings and were sold, as I understand, for very considerable sums.*

At the time of writing, the property consists of one large house with a small cottage, Vine Cottage, to the south. It seems slowly to be returning to its original form of a single house.

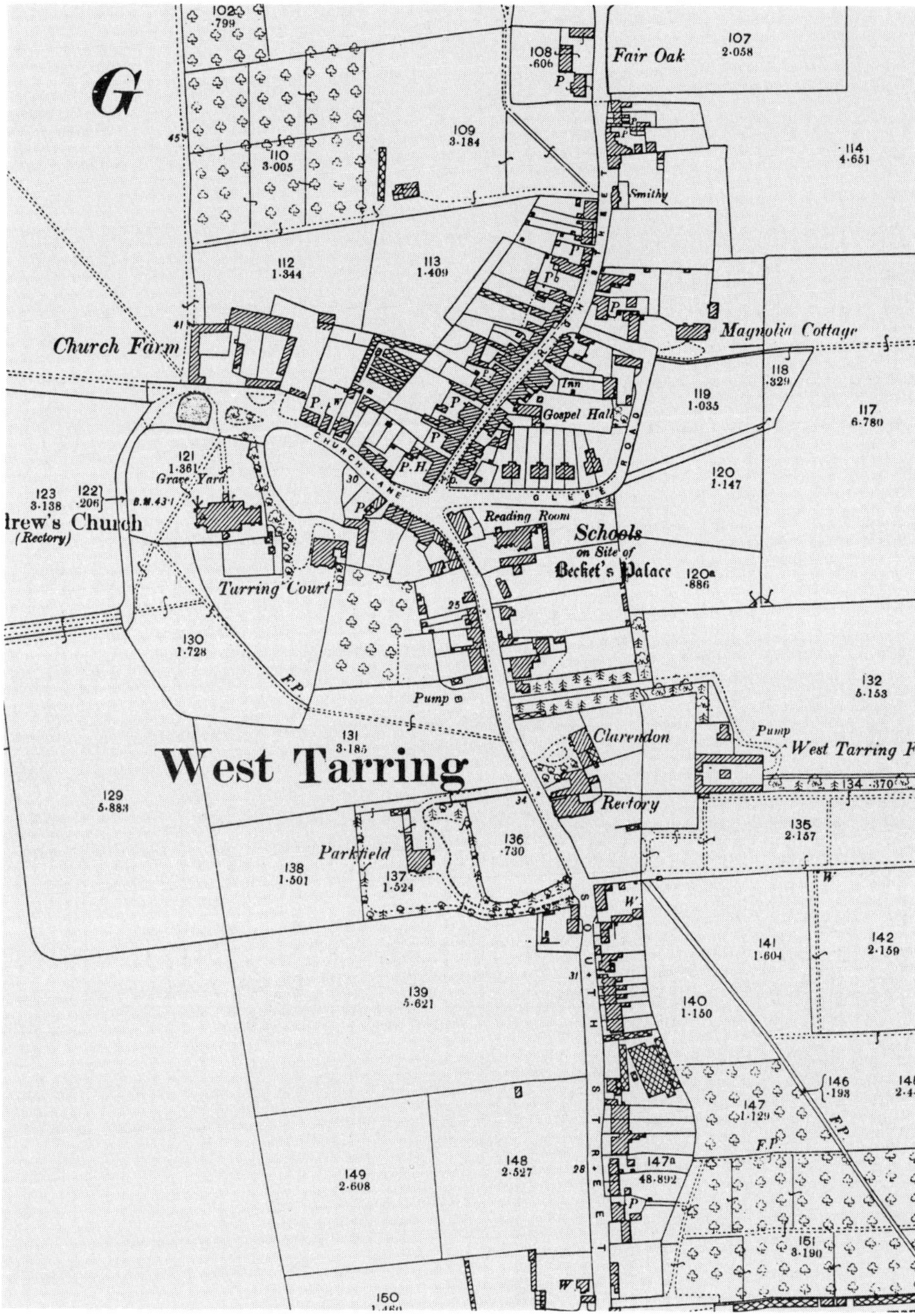


*32. The village of Tarring in 1898.*

CHAPTER SIX

# THE OLD CASTLE

As its name and the lamp above the door suggest, this house was at one time an inn. In 1638, there was just a cottage on the site, owned by Thomas Botting, and by 1660 there is reference to an orchard adjacent, presumably in what is now the garden.

*33. The Old Castle, which stands on the site of an earlier cottage, dates from the seventeenth century. It was an inn between 1762 and 1911.*

Botting bought the house from John Watersfield, who moved to Heene. The frailty of life at the time is shown by an order of the quarter session [50] of 1642:

*It is ordered that Richard Greenfield administrator of John Watersfield during the minority of Mary Watersfield daughter of the sayd John shall forthwith pay to William Cooke one of the overseers of the poore of Heene a member of the parish of Tarring the summe of Five pounds by him and the other overseer of the poore there disbursed for the reliefe of the said Mary and for the buriall of the said John and Mary his wife and two of theire children they all dying of the infectious disease of the plague as is supposed, as for the Inning of the Corne of the said John, he dying in harvest time.*

In 1717, it became part of the Penfold estate and was normally let. By this time, the house also had stables attached. On April 5th 1762, an advertisement appeared in the Sussex Weekly Advertiser:

*To be sold to the best bidder*
*On Monday the 12th instant, at the Castle, in*
*West Tarring in this county,*
*A Copyhold Messuage, Stable, Slaughter House, Garden*
*and Premises, in the North Street in West Tarring*
*aforesaid, formerly let to a butcher and now lately*
*used as a Publick House, and very convenient for both.*

This is undoubtedly a reference to the sale of the Castle itself, since the description is identical to that used in all subsequent manor court proceedings, and it is the only slaughterhouse regularly referred to in the village. We can be sure that the Castle first opened its doors for business as an inn in the years just prior to 1762.

Quite what happened at the sale is not clear, perhaps nobody turned up, but there is no record of a sale of the premises in the court rolls until five years later. What is certain is that it continued as an inn, and was often let. In 1798, it was described, along with the George, as *a good inn.*

By 1839, it was in the hands of Richard Tamplin, who had something of a monopoly of the licensed trade in Tarring at the time. He also owned the George, and his main competition, the Black Lion, which we shall discover later, had recently closed its doors.

This was probably not a very satisfactory state of affairs, but it was soon rectified with the arrival of Richard Parsons to open the Vine Brewery in 1843. During this period, drunkenness in Tarring was in decline, judging by the comments of the vicar [51] in 1860:

*When I first came into this country* (in 1834) *it was no uncommon thing to see drunkards reeling about the streets .... of this old decayed town ... It is now the rarest thing in the world, and it is two years since I have seen a person reeling drunk in public.*

The Castle was run as an inn by the Norris family, father, then mother, then son, for 45 years from 1866 until it finally closed its doors in 1911 and became a private house.

All of the houses from here down to and including number 16, Providence Cottage, stand on the site of a tenement called Cotmans. The name describes a class of tenant of a relatively small plot of land in the early Middle Ages, and this suggests the site is very old. This would be consistent with the outward spread of the village from its origins, centred on the Old Palace and the church.

In 1610, a house with an orchard and an acre of ground here was owned by Alice Humphrey, and the list of subsequent owners contains many old Tarring names, including Nye, Penfold, Parsons, Margesson, Pelling and Holcombe.

In 1787, John Pelling sold 44 ½ feet of frontage on the south of the site to Stephen Young, including a half share of the well and necessary house (an appropriate euphemism for an outside lavatory) in the garden at the back. By 1793, Young had divided his plot into two again, and sold the two parts separately with even smaller shares of the well and necessary. Providence Cottage probably dates from around this time.

A contemporary cottage attached to the north wall of Providence Cottage remained in 1839, but was replaced by a Plymouth Brethren Chapel, which was registered in 1860. In 1878, the chapel was described as a Christian Brethren Meeting House, and as Tarring Gospel Hall it still stands here today.

The three cottages to the north of the Gospel Hall are also probably contemporary with Providence Cottage, although it is possible they include remnants of Alice Humphrey's original house of 1610. Three hundred years later, the Humphreys were back in occupation, when Miss Kate Humphreys lived and worked here at number 20 as a dressmaker.

Number 22 is called Chippers Cottage, and understandably so, since it was occupied by members of the Chipper family continuously from 1839 to 1958. In that year, George Chipper died here at the age of 84 [52]. He had been crippled by polio as a child, and he worked all his long life here as a tailor, having been brought up by his aunt, Fanny Chipper, who ran the bakery opposite which later became the village store. Number 24 was also occupied for a time by a Chipper family at the turn of the century.

The land to the south of Providence Cottage, south to the Old Coach House, and east to Rectory Road, comprises the manor of Tarring Rectory, which has been separated from the manor of Tarring with Marlpost since the sixteenth century. The records of the rectory manor are not very extensive, and while we can discover quite a lot about the older and grander buildings on this land, information about the age and ownership of the ordinary cottages is hard to come by.

In 1839, there appears from the tithe map to have been a single house on the site of numbers 12 and 14, but it, together with the garden to the south and east, is described as *stables, yard &c* in the apportionment. The discrepancy between this and the tithe map could perhaps be explained if these two houses were in course of construction in 1839, and this would be consistent with their appearance. They have always been private houses. When an old building, which stood in the garden behind number 12, was demolished in around 1875, the house was extended at the rear. A further small house is shown on the tithe map adjacent to the north wall of Parsonage Row, but this had been demolished by 1875.

The terrace of houses from here south to the post office is known as Parsonage Row, and dates almost certainly from the fifteenth century [53], despite regular more extravagant claims. The post office itself, and number 4 next door, have been modernised in the same way as many other timber-framed houses in the street, but the effect can be seen particularly clearly here, since there are unaltered houses in the same terrace. On the ground floor, the process gave rise to very thick walls, embracing the upper storey overhang, and the tile hanging above is fixed directly to the timber frame.

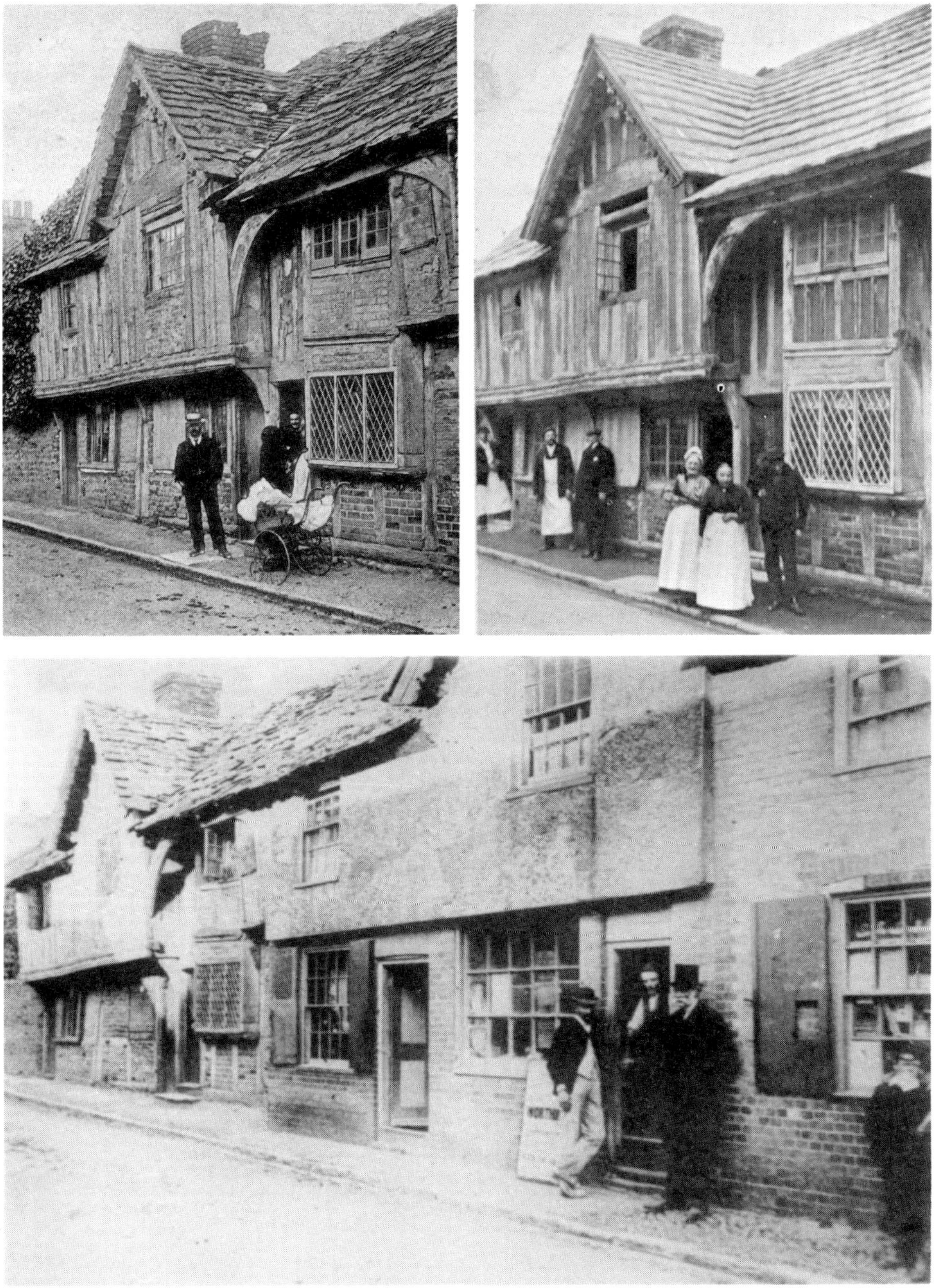

*34. Three photographs from early in the present century, showing Tarring people standing outside Parsonage Row.*

*35. A watercolour of Parsonage Row, painted by Mrs W.E.Partridge in about 1841, shows the southern section before it fell into disrepair. It was demolished in 1895.*

Parsonage Row originally extended further to the south [54], comprising a small medieval butcher's shop, and a further gabled house, but these were demolished in 1895 to make way for Glebe Road. Even in those days before the modern conservation movement had developed, the demolition of the butcher's shop was seen as a great loss, since surviving examples of mediaeval shop fronts are extremely rare. It can just be seen in the earliest photographs of Parsonage Row, and a line drawing has survived which gives a good impression of how it looked. To the south of the extended building was a gateway, through which sheep were admitted to the glebe meadow beyond.

*36. A detailed line drawing of the old butcher's shop, which was part of the section of Parsonage Row demolished in 1895.*

There is a record of repairs to a building on what seems to be this site [55] in 1505, as follows:

| | |
|---|---|
| For taking down stone of gatehouse | 6d |
| Ditto. Timber for same | 17s |
| Item. To the carpenter for making of new work, and laying in new timber in the old work, and the making of the buttery and 8 window pieces, with a stair | 14s5d |
| To the stone helyer | 11s6d |
| For the mending of the gearwear | 6d |
| For 3 quarters of lime | 4s8d |
| For carrying same | 1d |
| For fetching 4 loads of square timber and 7 loads of timber from the Maryll post, carried every load 20d | 18s4d |
| To John Mechell for carrying etc. for timber etc | ... |
| nails and so forth | ... |
| Total | 116s9d |

Since Parsonage Row has been dated architecturally to between 1480 and 1500, it is possible that this account relates to the construction of the present building as a major refurbishment of a previous structure.

The building as it now stands has three bays on two floors, the upper floor projecting by almost half a metre. The central bay is decorated with ornate barge boards, and is unusual in that it contains a hall on the upper floor. The windows do not of course date from as early as the fifteenth century, but appear to occupy the same positions as the original, smaller windows. The same is probably true of the chimneys.

*37. Parsonage Row looking south just before 1895. The southernmost gable can be seen to have lost its roof, and it was demolished soon after this photograph was taken.*

The whole building has been substantially extended at the back, but the facade, which shows great craftsmanship, looks now very much as it must have done five hundred years ago. Considerably less care was exercised by the builders on the interior, which is characterised

*38. The top photograph shows the High Street looking north before the demolition of the southern end of Parsonage Row. The mediaeval butcher's shop can be seen in the foreground. The lower, modern photograph was taken from the same viewpoint.*

by very roughly sawn timbers. This suggests that the original construction was ornamental, rather than as a dwelling for a wealthy man.

It has been speculated that the original purpose of the building was as an impressive entrance to the Old Palace. It is certainly a possibility, consistent with the upper floor hall, and the concentration on external appearance rather than internal craftsmanship. A further piece of circumstantial evidence dates from 1615, when the building was described [56] as *a certayne Tenemente called the Parsonage Gates.* It would certainly have made an impressive entrance, the more so since the building was in a street of village houses of much less spectacular design. By 1749, the tenement was owned by a lady with the delightful name of Love Haines.

Because of the existence of numerous old postcards showing the post office here, it is usually assumed that it has been here since it opened [57] in 1871. This is not so however, since it was operated from Market Building across the street for a period between 1910 and 1935. It is also not the original office, since a postmaster is recorded at number 25 as long ago as 1798. The shop was also a bakery before it became a confectioner's. Maybe it was forced to change by the strength of competition, since this is the fourth baker's shop we have discovered at this end of the street during the last century.

In 1850, Tarring was still an important town, and people came here from Worthing to shop. Even early in this century, it was common to walk across the fields to Tarring to buy home-made bread [58]. The baking was carried out in a building to the south, on the site of the reading room, which was originally the episcopal brewhouse [59]. It was demolished in the late nineteenth century.

The building just behind the post office in Glebe Road, now a garage with a rather unattractive asbestos roof, is older than it looks. It was originally the slaughterhouse which served the little butcher's shop. In around 1856, the ovens were moved here from the old brewhouse [60], and it became the bakery. Mrs Longley, who kept the post office at the turn of the century, remembered people bringing their Sunday pies here to be baked.

At this time the entrance to this building was on the north side, and when Glebe Road was cut, the old bakehouse presented a blank flint

*39. The old bakehouse in 1929, and as it looks, much altered, today.*

wall to the street. In 1929, after the bakery had closed, it was partly demolished, but the side walls were retained, and the building, now facing in the opposite direction, found yet another use as a garage.

The house immediately to the north of the post office has a long connection with shoemaking. Thomas Binstead lived and worked here as a cobbler from 1866 to 1895, and was succeeded by George Greenyer, who later moved to premises on the other side of the street. Earlier, in 1855, Thomas, a bootmaker and yet another member of the Chipper family, is recorded in Tarring and possibly worked here.

When an old well in the garden of the post office was excavated [61] in 1961, a substantial volume of cobbler's waste was discovered, which had been used to fill in the well in the period between 1490 and 1510. It had presumably ceased to be used as a well following the construction of Parsonage Row, when a new well at a more convenient location would have been dug. The pieces of leather found in the well were for the most part very badly worn, the uppers being damaged across the front, the heels worn down, and some of the soles so badly holed that they must have been worn for some time after they first wore through. All in all, the evidence suggests that the cobbler's customers in the sixteenth century were poor indeed.

The timber-framed northern section of Parsonage Row has survived plans for demolition in the present century. For many years it was a small museum owned by the Sussex Archaeological Trust, but eventually they too found it too expensive to maintain. The Borough Council narrowly voted not to buy the property, and it passed into private hands, to be converted into a restaurant.

There was considerable controversy at the time that it would spoil the atmosphere of the street, but the conversion has been delicately handled, and we can be sure the fabric will now be maintained in good repair. Even so, there are far fewer commercial premises in the High Street now than there ever have been before, and the houses are in a much better state of repair than at any previous time.

In 1900, for instance, there were, in the street, a baker at Banner House, a bootmaker at number 13, and possibly also at number 4, a grocer at number 19, a furniture dealer at number 23, the post office and sweetshop at number 2, another bakery at Chippers Cottage, a coal merchant and fly proprietor at number 30, a coachbuilder on the

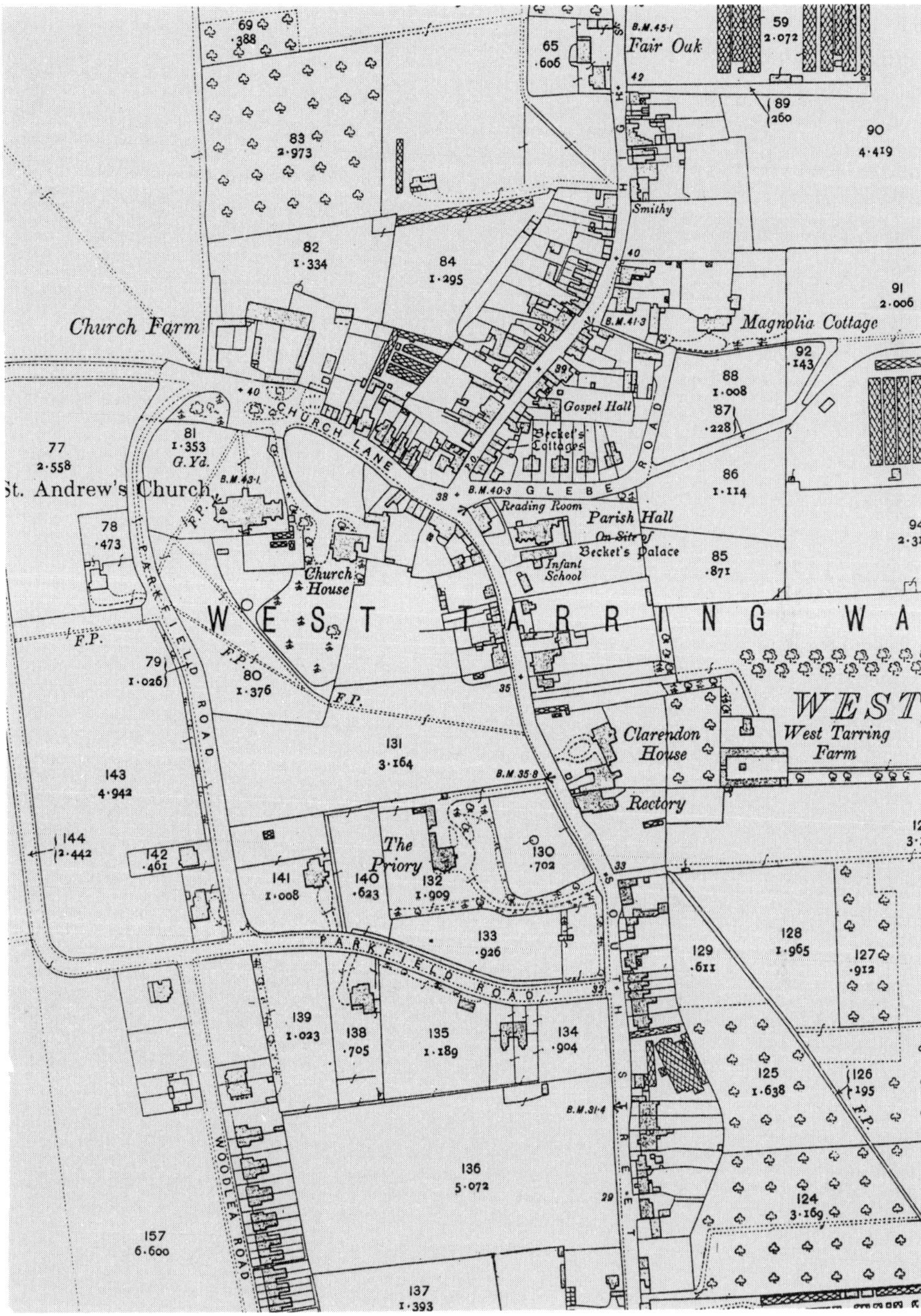


40. *The village of Tarring in 1912.*

site of the Vine car park, and, of course, the rapidly growing Hollands' smithy on the site of Dorset Place. In addition there was a beer retailer at the Vine, and two public houses. Even in 1946, there were still six shops, the George and Dragon, a joinery factory and two garages. Now, we find only two inns, the post office and the Parsonage Restaurant.

Standing here, in the old market-place of Tarring, take a look up the street. From the post office to The Hollies, and from the George to the Vine, the view is not much different to that of 150 years ago. The street has been surfaced with tarmac, and the pavements paved. The piles of horse manure have been replaced by cars, and there are street lights, but otherwise, very little has changed.

In this, Tarring is a special village. There are many places with older houses, and many houses as old which have been better preserved, but in Sussex, it is unusual to find a whole street which is as little changed in 150 years as the High Street we have just walked along.

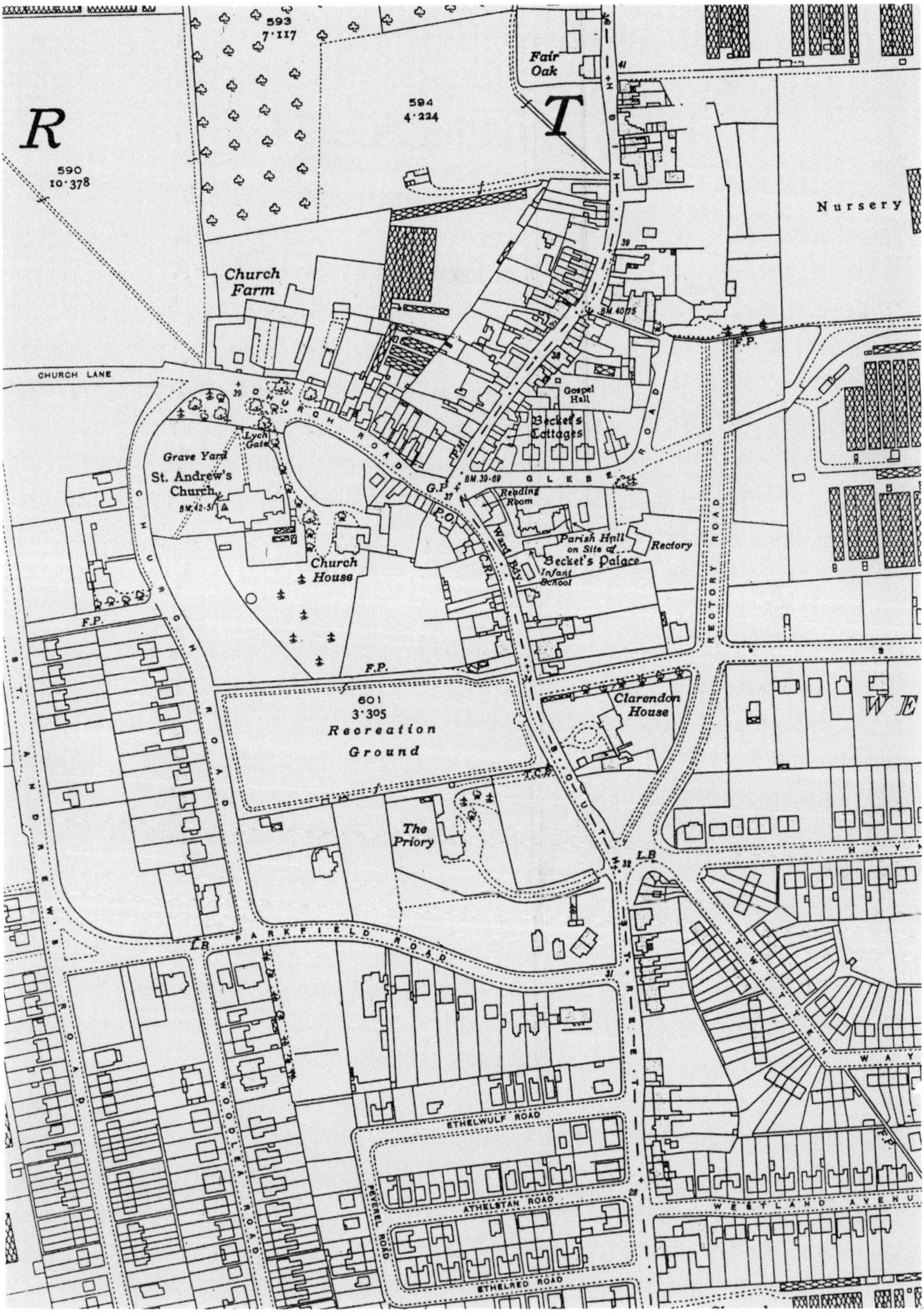


*41. The village of Tarring in 1932.*

CHAPTER SEVEN

# THE OLD PALACE

As we have now arrived at the oldest surviving part of the village, we should perhaps look back at its early history.

The first evidence of habitation [62] in this area is found in the flint implements made by old stone age man in the Palaeolithic era, over 100,000 years ago. The climate here then was warm, perhaps subtropical, and these people lived by hunting and fishing. They had not learned to domesticate animals nor to cultivate crops. They were nomadic, and wandered over the coastal plain, which was probably considerably wider from down to sea than it is today.

Over the centuries, the climate gradually became colder, and although these primitive creatures would not have recognised it, or even noticed the change over a single lifetime, the last ice-age was arriving. As the ice-cap moved imperceptibly but inexorably south, the sea level fell, and the English Channel narrowed. Eventually, the glaciers reached the Thames valley, and the Channel became a narrow river. The climate here was sub-arctic, driving the nomadic people far to the south, across the river into France. The land was cold, barren and deserted, and so it remained for 30,000 years.

Eventually, though, the ice began to retreat. By this time, Palaeolithic man had been ousted from France by the new breed Homo Sapiens, and as the climate slowly improved, so the land around Tarring received its first exploratory visits from Mesolithic men, returning across the river which their Palaeolithic predecessors had crossed 30,000 years before.

The melting ice slowly raised the level of the sea, and as the river gradually widened, our intrepid visitors had to detour farther and farther to the east to find a safe crossing. Eventually, some seven or eight thousand years ago, they found the river unfordable, and some of them became marooned on the new island of Great Britain.

From that time on, the land has been continuously occupied, with the nomadic lifestyle of the Mesolithic castaways being influenced by wave after wave of foreign invaders.

Five thousand years ago, Neolithic men came from the Mediterranean to the south west of England. They built the great stone circles of Stonehenge and Avebury, and introduced agriculture, domestic animals and flint mining to Sussex. They were the first inhabitants to make permanent settlements here, and they dug hundreds of mines on Cissbury Hill and elsewhere to extract flints to make their tools.

The process of mining flints consisted of digging vertical shafts into the downland chalk using tools made from deer antlers and ox bones. Eventually, at a depth of between three and twelve metres, a seam of flint was reached, and galleries were cut in all directions to follow the seam. The largest flint mines so far discovered in this country are at Grimes Graves in Norfolk and have been partly excavated.A visit there shows dramatically how hard and dangerous the work must have been. The mines at Cissbury are second only to Grimes Graves in size, and together with smaller operations at Harrow Hill, Church Hill Findon, Tolmere Pond Findon, and Blackpatch Hill near Myrtlegrove, constituted a major local industry.

It was necessary to mine flints in this way since only when they were recovered directly from the chalk could they be flaked into tools. Flint nodules found on the surface, having suffered from extended exposure to the elements, are almost impossible to work, as anyone who has tried it will know.

Later, invaders from Belgium and northern France brought with them the technology to make bronze, and we know that in this period there were two farms in Findon.

A thousand years later, in the millenium before Christ, Celts from the west introduced iron working, and built the first towns in the area, at Cissbury and Highdown. As well as being home for the flint workers, these fortified hills provided refuge for farmers of the surrounding land from attack by other tribes.

In 71 BC, a tribe of the Belgae, from the continent, invaded and occupied the far west of Sussex, and from their base in a now lost town near Chichester, held sway over the lands of Tarring. Sixteen years later, Julius Caesar led the first Roman invasion of Britain.

Caesar's own record of the invasion constitutes one of the earliest written historical sources in English history. He described how the native Britons dyed themselves with a blue dye called woad, and shaved all their bodies except their heads and upper lips. Wives were shared between groups of ten to twelve men, often brothers or fathers and sons [63].

The brief punitive visit of the Romans in 55 BC was followed by a further sortie in the following year. It was not until AD 43, however, under the direction of the stuttering Emperor Claudius, that the Romans really began their occupation of England. By this time, King Verica [64] ruled Sussex, and was among the first to transfer his allegience to the invaders. As a result, he was confirmed as ruler by the Romans. His successor, King Cogidubnus, was a great friend of Rome, and was granted the rare honour of being made a Roman citizen.

Cogidubnus was responsible for much of the construction of Roman Chichester, and although the walls have since been rebuilt, they stand on the site of the original Roman ones. He built an amphitheatre, which unfortunately was built over in the 1930's, and also a temple dedicated to Neptune and Minerva. The dedication stone, recording that the temple was indeed commissioned by Cogidubnus, can still be seen in Chichester at the entrance to the Guildhall. Under his rule and subsequently, Sussex prospered.

The A27 road from Chichester to Pevensey was built by the Romans [65], probably along the line of an existing track, and along its length, villas and other buildings were constructed. The magnificent palace at Fishbourne was the largest private Roman residence that has been found in England. It covered over four acres of ground, roughly the same area as Buckingham Palace covers today, and was probably built for Cogidumnus himself. In addition to this and the other well-known villa at Bignor, a villa has been excavated at Angmering, and more recently another has been discovered in the grounds of Northbrook College. A bathhouse has been excavated at Highdown. There was a villa on the site of Worthing Library in Chapel Road, and another on the eastern side of Grand Avenue, between Mill Road and Lansdowne Road. Evidence of Roman occupation has also been found at the southern end of Ringmer Road [66].

With elegant villas spread out along the coast [67] - more than 40 have been discovered in the county - and scattered groups of peasant farmers' huts, Roman Sussex must have been a pleasant and prosperous place, but it was not to last.

By AD 400, the Roman Empire was beginning to collapse. Faced with growing invasion threats on several fronts in Europe, the Emperor Honorius was forced to withdraw his troops from Britain and abandon the land once more to its native inhabitants. Deprived of the protection of the Roman legions the land was defenceless, and within a century, the Saxon raiders who were commonplace along the coast had begun to settle on the fertile coastal plain, ousting the Celts.

These Saxons made an impression on the environment which can still be perceived today. Whereas the Celts had lived in scattered houses on the higher ground of the Downs, the Saxons lived in what we would recognise as villages, close groups of houses surrounded by cultivated fields. It is likely that this period marks the first appearance of a village settlement at Tarring.

Certainly the name is a Saxon one, meaning *Teorra's people* [68], and the coastal plain between the Adur and the Arun has a greater concentration of Saxon place names than anywhere else in Sussex - Poling, Angmering, Ferring, Goring, Durrington, Salvington, Lancing, Sompting and Worthing are all names of Saxon origin.

In addition, of course, the name Sussex derives from the home of the South Saxons. The arrival of the Saxons is documented in the Anglo Saxon Chronicles [69] for the year AD 477:

*In this year Aelle came to Britain and his three sons Cymen, and Wlencing, and Cissa with three ships at the place which is called Cymenesora, and there slew many Welsh and drove some in flight into the wood which is called Andredesleg.*

This quotation needs some explanation. Cymenesora was a place to the south of the present Selsey Bill, the Welsh refers to the indigenous Celtic inhabitants, and Andredesleg was the vast forest which covered the Weald of Sussex, the area between the North and the South Downs.

By the year 607 the inhabitants are referred to as the South Saxons, and in 661 we find the first reference to Sussex:

*Wulfhere, son of Penda, committed ravage on Wight, and gave the people of Wight to Aethelwald, king of Sussex, because Wulfhere had received him at baptism. And Eoppa, the mass-priest, by order of Wilfrith and king Wulfhere, first brought baptism to the people of Wight.*

The Chronicles were written in English, although not a form that we would easily recognise today, since the language did not then contain any words of French origin. They provide an amazing story of continual inter-tribal war over the following centuries, interspersed with records of natural events. Some arbitrary extracts give a flavour:

*664. In this year the sun was eclipsed on the vth of the Nones of May* (May 3). *In the same year there was a great pestilence in the island of Britain.*

*685. In this year there was bloody rain in Britain, and milk and butter were turned to blood.*

*722. In this year queen Aethelburgh destroyed Taunton, which Ine had previously built; and Ealdberht the exile withdrew into Surrey and Sussex.*

*725. and Ine fought against the South Saxons, and there slew Ealdbriht, the atheling whom he had before driven out.*

*773. In this year a red cross appeared in the heavens after sunset...and wondrous serpents were seen in the South Saxons' land.*

*787. And in these days first came three ships of Northmen from Haeretha land: and then the reeve rode thereto and would drive them to the king's vill, for he knew not what they were, and they there slew him. Those were the first ships of Danish men that sought the land of the English race.*

This last entry marks the commencement of over two centuries of harassment of the country by the Danes, which was not to be relieved until 1017. The Chronicles paint a vivid picture:

*793. In this year dire forewarnings came over the land of the Northumbrians, and miserably terrifed the inhabitants: these were excessive whirlwinds and lightenings, and fiery dragons were seen flying in the air: a great famine soon followed these tokens, and a little after that in the same year on the vith of the Ides of January* (January 8) *the havoc of heathen men miserably destroyed God's church in Lindisfarne through rapine and slaughter.*

*837. In this year ealdorman Wulfheard fought at Southampton against the crews of thirty-three ships, and there made great slaughter, and gained the victory; and in the same year the aldorman Aethelhelm fought against a Danish army at Portland with the Dorset men, and for a good while put the army to flight, but the Danes held possession of the battle place, and slew the aldorman.*

*855. In this year the heathen men first took up their quarters over winter in Sheppey.*

*897. Thanks be to God, the army had not utterly broken up the Angle race; but they were much more severely broken in those three years by a mortality of cattle and of men, most of all thereby that many of the king's most excellent thanes that were in the land died in those three years: one of these was ...Eadulf, a king's thane in Sussex.*

*In the same year the armies from the East Angles and Northumbrians harassed the West Saxons' land, very much on the south coast, by predatory bands, most of all by the long ships which they had built many years before. Then king Alfred commanded long ships to be built against them, which were full nigh twice as long as the others, some had sixty oars, some more; they were both swifter and steadier, and also higher than the others.*

*Then on a certain time in the same year, there came six ships to Wight, and did there much evil, both in Devon and elsewhere on the seashore. Then the king commanded to go thither with nine of the new ships, and they blockaded against them the mouth into the outer sea. Then they went with three ships out against them, and three lay high up in the mouth in the dry: the men were gone off on shore.*

*Then they took two of the three ships at the outward mouth, and slew the men, and the one escaped, in which also all the men were killed, save five who came away because the ships of the others were aground. They were also aground very inconveniently; three were aground on the side of the deep on which the Danish ships were aground, and all the others on the other side, so that not one of them could get to the others. But, when the water had ebbed many furlongs from the ships, then the Danish went from the three ships to the other three which had been left by the ebb on their side, and they then fought there. There were slain...Frisian and English,sixty-two, and of the Danish one hundred and twenty.*

*But then the flood came to the Danish ships, before the Christians could shove theirs out, and they therefore rowed away out; They were then so damaged that they could not row round the South Saxons' land, for there the sea cast two of them on land, and the men were led to the king at Winchester, and he commanded them to be there hanged. In the same summer no less than twenty ships, with men and everything, perished on the south coast.*

I make no apology for this extended excerpt from the Anglo Saxon Chronicles. Among the earliest of historical descriptive narratives, they illustrate vividly the nature of the times, from which the people of Tarring would not have been immune. Tarring would almost certainly have had a wooden church by this time, and almost as surely we can assume it would have been burned to the ground at least once by Danish raiders.

In the year 923, Athelstan became King, and shortly before his death in 939, he granted the lands of Tarring to the estate of the cathedral at Canterbury. The original charter has been lost, but a thirteenth century copy of a subsequent charter exists, in which King Edmund, Athelstan's successor, confirmed the grant [70]:

*This return was made in the year in which Aethelstan the brother of King Edmund and of Eadred died, who nevertheless before his death gave to the aforesaid church of Christ already mentioned one town called Terringes situate by the sea in Suthsexe. And the same year the aforesaid Edmund was raised to the throne, and freed the aforesaid lands from all secular dues and official taxation, except for the raising of troops and the building of bridges and forts.*

Thus began the association of Tarring with the Archbishop of Canterbury which was to last until the middle of the nineteenth century. Unfortunately for inhabitants of present day Tarring, the blanket exemption from tax which was granted has been repealed by subsequent legislation!

The ravaging of this coast by the Danes continued during the tenth century, and was finally abated only by the choice of the Danish invader Cnut as King of England in 1017. This was the King Canute who is reputed to have tried to turn back the tide: some say at Bosham. Following Cnut's death in 1035, unrest resumed within the country and foreign invaders returned.

In 1066, King Harold had just scored a major victory over a Norwegian invasion force when news reached him of the invasion by William the Bastard from Normandy, an event which was to have lasting consequences not just for Tarring and Sussex, but for the country as a whole.

King Harold force marched his army from Yorkshire to Hastings, and hurriedly sought reinforcements from the surrounding countryside. Two years earlier, when Harold had visited William in Normandy, he had stayed en route at the manor house of Earl Godwin at Bosham. It seems likely, therefore, that when the call went out to the men of Sussex to gather at an ancient apple tree outside Hastings, men from Bosham would have been among the first to respond. Since their route to Hastings was through the parish of Tarring, we can safely assume that Tarring men joined them on their march, and stood beside the King in that fateful battle.

A major priority for William after his victory was to secure control of the Sussex coast, which gave him access to his homeland of Normandy. Accordingly, he divided the county into five regions, called Rapes, based on Chichester, Arundel, Bramber, Lewis and Hastings. Each was entrusted to one of William's faithful barons, and from a strong castle, each controlled a seaport and a road to the north.

Tarring stood in Bramber Rape, under the control of William de Braose, although the manor itself remained in the control of the Archbishop of Canterbury. The river Adur at this time was much wider and navigable up to Bramber and Steyning, and the port at Shoreham lay considerably to the north of the present harbour.

As Sussex settled down under its new masters, William the Conqueror set about making the famous survey of his lands known as the Domesday book. Here we find a second reference to Tarring [71]:

*The Archbishop himself holds Terringes, which always belonged to the Monastery. In the time of King Edward it vouched for 18 hides, now for 7 hides and one virgate. There is land for 14 ploughs and one half. In demesne are 3 ploughs; and 27 villeins with 14 bordars have 10 ploughs. There are 2 churches, and wood for 6 hogs. In the time of King Edward it was worth £14 4s, and afterwards £10. Now £15. Of this manor William de Braose holds four hides, and has there in demesne 1 plough; and 4 villeins with 5 bordars have 1 plough and a half. There are 5 acres of meadow. Of wood 10 pence, of pannage 20s and 2 hogs. Worth 70 shillings.*

The reference to the monastery is not certain, although it probably relates to the monks at Canterbury who dealt with the affairs of the archbishop. There were apparently monks in Tarring [72] in 1189, when they petitioned the archbishop during one of his visits for permission to go to the King - for what purpose is not known - and to return in safety. A hospital dedicated to St Mary [73], normally a monastic institution at the time, was recorded in 1277.

The hide and the virgate were Saxon measures of land. A hide comprised one hundred Saxon acres, or roughly 125 modern acres, but the size of a virgate is rather less certain [74].

It should be remembered, of course, that this was a survey for taxation purposes, and so only taxable land would have been recorded. Nevertheless, the 18 hides before 1066 would amount to 2250 modern acres, almost exactly twice the size of Tarring in the sixteenth and in the nineteenth centuries. We know that the Domesday manor included the land at Marlpost, but excluded Heene and Salvington, so it seems likely to have included other land as well. It is possible that some of this additional land was lost to the sea subsequently, as there are several records of such loss of land in the later records [75].

Demesne land, as we have seen, was land directly under the control of the lord of the manor, rather than sublet. Villeins were holders of substantial pieces of land, and bordars of lesser amounts, perhaps five acres each. Pannage, the right to release pigs and other animals to graze in the woodland of the manor, probably relates to the outlying land at Marlpost.

One of the churches mentioned is surely that of Tarring. This was probably a wooden structure, and no trace of it remains today, although most likely it occupied the same site as the present church. The second church is more of a puzzle. The most likely explanation is that it represents a long destroyed church belonging to Heene but situated in Tarring manor. The Domesday record for Heene makes no reference to a church, and Heene did subsequently become part of the rectory of Tarring.

At a value of £15, the Tarring of 1086 was a relatively large village in the area. Locally, only Findon was larger in value. Patching, Broadwater and Lancing were of similar size, but the other villages close by - Ferring, Goring, Salvington, Clapham, Offington, Heene, Durrington and Worthing (then the two manors of Ordinges and Mordinges), all mentioned in the Domesday book, were of much lower value.

We now come to the Old Palace itself. The earliest surviving parts of the structure have been dated at around 1230, although there are traces of subsequent extension or rebuilding in almost every subsequent century.

The oldest part of the structure is the rectangular hall at the east end of the building, farthest away from the present main door [76]. When originally built the living quarters consisted of a single room, or hall, situated on the upper floor. This was approached by an external staircase, built of stone, and probably situated where the present internal doorway leads to this hall. The ground floor contained storage space and shelters for animals.

In around 1300, the building was substantially extended by the construction of the larger room, with a single storey. The hall was widened in the fifteenth century, and the windows enlarged and modernised. It was also at this time that the door at the western end was added. Further additions and alterations have made it even harder to imagine the building as it was in the thirteenth century, when a dispute arose.

Although the archbishop owned the manor of Tarring, he had been in the habit of leasing it out in return for cash or services, and in 1237 it was let to Godfrey le Waleys. Godfrey was accused of mistreating the tenants, and was deprived of the manor until a fine of £80, an

*42. The Old Palace looks much the same today as it did in 1791, when the top drawing was made. The gable on the left was built originally in about 1230 to stand alone as a hall with a single room situated on the first floor.*

enormous sum in those days, had been paid. Forty years later, Godfrey's grandson Richard was also in trouble for mistreating the tenants, and this time the case was brought before the King's court. The records of the court of King Edward I for May 7th 1277 at Westminster record the dispute in detail [77]:

*The assise comes to know whether the archbishop, Adam de Wendelesworth, Andrew de Jarpenvill, John de Arderne and Master Roger de Dertford disseised the said Richard (Richard le Waleys, knight) of his free tenement in Terring, to wit, of two parts of the manor of Terring, except 28 acres of land. The archbishop comes not, but Richard de Pevense, his bailiff, comes, and Adam, Andrew, John and Roger come. The archbishop, by his bailiffs, says that the assise should not proceed because he entered with the will of Richard, who gave him the keys of the manor: that Richard holds the manor at his will by the service of £18 yearly in money or its value at the option of the archbishop, who shall come there once a year if he wishes and stay there until he should consume food and other necessaries to that amount, or at the four terms, and consume a fourth part, on condition of giving 40 days notice.*

*In allowance of the said £18, he shall find for the archbishop a quarter of wheat for 18d, a quarter of oats for 8d, 4 gallons of best ale for 1d, and if it be and if the ale be not the best let the cask be smashed, the ale spilt, and 1d or ½d put on the cask, a fat ox carcase for 16d, a male pig over a year old and of reasonable size for 8d, a fat mutton carcase for 4d, two fat geese for 1d, four fat hens for 1d, a hundred of eggs for 1d and another hundred for nothing, dishes, plates, salt-cellars, cups, skewers, firewood, coal, salt, pychers daily at noon, hay for nothing, and litter likewise for nothing. He shall keep the men of the manor according to their tenures, and as freely without vexation and exaction as the archbishop keeps his men of his other manors, under pain of losing his manor, and if he fails, the archbishop may enter the manor and keep it at will.*

*And because Richard, when the archbishop came to the manor to take the service in kind as above, expended £6 17s 5¾d only and defaulted as to the residue of service, and also vexes the men of the manor and exacts from them other customs and services than he ought or than the archbishop exacts from his men in other of his manors, the archbishop took the manor into his hands, as was lawful for him to do.*

After much delay, and twice consulting the King, the jury ruled in favour of the archbishop and Richard willingly gave up the manor to him.

Of course, exact comparisons are not possible, but it is interesting to compare the costs of some of these commodities with their approximate equivalents seven hundred years later. The 1282 custumal [78] gave us a value of ½d for one day's manual farm labour, or 3d for a six day week, compared to the minimum weekly wage for unskilled farm labourers in 1989 of £112.02. Using these figures we can compare not only absolute prices, but also the number of hours work required then and now to purchase the commodities listed:

| COMMODITY | 1277 | | 1990 | |
|---|---|---|---|---|
| | *PRICE* | *HOURS WORK* | *PRICE [79]* | *HOURS WORK* |
| quarter[1] of wheat | 18d | 360 | £22.50 | 10 |
| quarter of oats | 8d | 160 | £40.00 | 17 |
| gallon of ale | ¼d | 5 | £7.00[2] | 3 |
| fat ox carcase | 16d | 320 | £650.00 | 279 |
| a pig | 8d | 160 | £80.00 | 34 |
| mutton carcase | 4d | 80 | £30.00 | 13 |
| a goose | ½d | 10 | £30.00 | 13 |
| a fat hen | ¼d | 5 | £5.00 | 2 |
| 100 eggs | ½d | 10 | £7.50 | 3 |

[1] - *the imperial British quarter, a measure of capacity for grain equal to 480 lbs.*
[2] - *excluding VAT and excise duty for a fairer comparison.*

On average, prices have increased five thousand times since 1277. This may seem a lot, but over more than seven hundred years it represents only just over one per cent per annum inflation. Over the same period, wages have risen nine thousand times, almost twice as much. Although the comparison is of course very rough, the table does give some indication of the improvement in the standard of living of the ordinary man over these seven hundred years. It also illustrates the transformation of the goose from a poor man's meat to a luxury, and the effects of the dramatic increase in the price of beef (ox) which has taken place in living memory.

*43. This drawing of the Old Palace from the south west shows the well which once stood in the garden.*

Returning to the dispute, the jury's ruling meant that the manor, with its newly built manor house, reverted to the archbishop, who reinstated the previous customs, as we have seen, in the custumal of 1282. Tarring remained in the estate of the Church in Canterbury until 1397, when Thomas Arundel, the then archbishop, forfeited the lands to the Crown. He had been banished by Parliament for treason, having plotted with the Duke of Gloucester, Henry Earl of Derby, and Richard Earl of Arundel, his brother, to overthrow King Richard II. The King sent an emissary to Tarring to make an inventory of the estate he had acquired, and the account has been preserved [80]. It shows that the site of the Palace covered three acres, which was broadly the same area as the Palace grounds in 1839, just before the tithe barns were sold off. The inventory gave a detailed list of the property of the manor, which is interesting in the way it illustrates the relative importance of farm impliments of the time:

*Thomas archbishop of Canterbury... had in right of his church in Canterbury the manor of Terryngge, in which there is a site with a garden of three acres in a close of no net yearly value, 280 acres of arable land worth 4d an acre yearly, pasture for 150 sheep worth 18d yearly, 30 acres of several pasture in the parish of Horsham belonging to the manor worth 2d an acre yearly, 10 acres of meadow worth 12d an acre yearly, a wood of about 7 acres of no net yearly value, £14 rents of assize of free and bond tenants, a windmill worth 20s net yearly and 75s 8d from divers small farms. On 25 September 21 Richard II* (1397) *he had there 3 stottes*(horses?) *worth 10s each, 24 oxen worth 12s each, a boar and three sows worth 20d each 30 small pigs worth 18d each, 3 ploughs with iron ropes and other gear worth 6s 8d, 2 long waggons with a set of wheels worth 6s 8d, 2 short waggons in poor condition with a set of wheels worth 4s, a curtepot*(?) *with wheels worth 20d, 3 harrows with wooden teeth, 2 fetropes*(?), *a dongeforke a shovele a spade and a mattok worth 2s in all, 3 sakkes worth 12d, an iron-bound bushel* (barrel) *worth 10d, 2 berlepes* (?) *and 3 sets of traces worth 9d, an estimated 90 quarters of wheat in sheaves worth 5s a quarter, 145 quarters of barley worth 3s 4d a quarter, 22 quarters of vetch worth 3s a quarter, 15 quarters of oats worth 2s a quarter and 2 cartloads of hay worth 6s 8d.*

When compared to the values in 1277, most seem to have increased by a factor of about three, and once again, over a period of 120 years this represents an annual rate of inflation of just over one per cent.

The manor was returned to Canterbury very soon afterwards, presumably after Archbishop Thomas had returned to England in 1399 to crown Henry Earl of Derby, one of his co-conspiritors, as Henry IV of England. The manor was later confiscated again by statute of Queen Elizabeth I in 1559. It may have been at this time that the manor was split into two, with the Palace, Parsonage Row and some adjacent land, now known as the Manor of Tarring Rectory, being returned to the archbishop, while the rest of the land remained in possession of the Crown. Both estates were initially leased out, although the Crown granted the larger estate to Sir William Garraway in 1616. An ecclesiastical return, or terrier [81], of 1615, describes the estate of the parsonage as follows:

*The parsonage hath a Mansion House by the selfe, and a certayne tenemente called the Parsonage Gates with an orchard and backside ajoining thereunto. Secondly, the said Parsonage in a field called the*

*Townfield hath ten acres of arable land belonging thereunto, though some say doth of right belong unto the vicarage.*

There seems little doubt that the mansion house in question was the present building, although the post of parson, or rector was what was called a sinecure. The incumbent had no duties, and so no need to live in the parish, but simply collected the tithes due to him, and rents from letting of the land and buildings.

44. *An old watercolour of the Palace showing the young village folk happy to be out of school.*

The Palace was in use as a school by 1779, having been repaired and converted by the rector, Jeremiah Miles. This was noted [82] in 1792:

> *The ruins of the old manerial house in which by tradition Thomas a'Becket stayed, still remain. The parish clerk, John Russell, an intelligent old man of 88 years of age, remembers it divided into three rooms, but the late rector, Dr Jeremiah Miles, Dean of Exeter, repaired it and threw the whole together for the purpose of a charity school.*

The school was run for 45 years by Daniel Monk, who was still alive in 1853 at the age of 94. It appears, though, that the school had fallen into disuse by this time, as the rector was anxious that it should be reopened as the parish school [83]. His ambition seems to have been fulfilled, and the building continued to be so used intermittently until 1985, when the reception classes of the Thomas a'Becket County Primary School were relocated from here to their present site in Bellview Road. An interesting little sidelight into the history of the building was uncovered in 1963 when a trench dug near the east wall of the building [84] was found to contain a large pit full of champagne bottles!

*45. The Old Palace as a school at the turn of the century.*

As we have seen, Parsonage Row cottages extended much farther to the south, leaving only a small gate between them and the cottages which stood on the site of the Parish Reading Room. These cottages were originally built as the episcopal brewhouse, which was reputed to date from the fourteenth century, and were demolished [85] in about 1890.

Directly ahead, in front of numbers 2 to 4 Glebe Road, and straddling the road in front of numbers 6 and 7, stood the rectorial tithe barns [86], used for storing the produce levied on the inhabitants of the parish by the rectory for their tithes. These were rendered obsolete by the commutation of tithes for cash payment in the years before 1839, and they were sold in 1840. By 1853 they had been demolished [87], and the present houses on the north side of Glebe Road had been built [88] by 1898. The eastern pair of these houses is set at an angle to the road, a permanent reminder that when it was originally built, the road was a cul-de-sac, turning north at this point on its way to Magnolia Cottage. These houses then stood four-square to the road.

On the south side of Glebe Road a new rectory was built when Rectory Road was cut in 1933, and the houses between this and the Palace were built, replacing a guide hut, in recent years.

CHAPTER EIGHT

# SOUTH STREET

The Parish Reading Room was built in 1891, and was presented to the parish for the use of artisans and labourers of the district. It was still being used for meetings, and as a classroom, until 1978 when the infants school moved to its present site in Bellview Road. The building also contained a small cottage. Previously, this was the site of the episcopal brasinium, or brewhouse, attached to the Palace, and reputedly dating from before 1397. Before it was demolished to make way for the new building, it had been divided into three cottages and a washhouse, where an old lady who lived in one of the cottages took in laundry.

The infants school also used the Old Palace as a classroom, but most of its activities took place in the building which now houses the dancing school, and which, despite its looks, dates back only as far as 1880.

The house next to the Reading Room is called The Old Coach House. Despite its name, it is not really old. There was no building here [89] in 1839, and the house was probable constructed [90] in around 1880. It was, however, originally a coach-house, and local residents can remember the large doors which graced its facade. After the coming of the motor car, it was used as a storehouse for many years, and was converted to residential use only recently.

The dovecote in the garden is over 150 years old, and may be very much older. Such buildings are difficult to date with any precision. It contains some 400 nesting boxes, and the entry point for the doves in the centre of the roof can be clearly seen. Until modern methods of husbandry were developed, many, sometimes most, of the larger domestic animals failed to survive the winter, so doves were often kept as a source of meat throughout the year.

In 1963, an excavation [91] in the garden on the north side of the coach-house revealed the remains of a mediaeval house, in use from the thirteenth to the sixteenth centuries. The earliest remains, which

*46. The Fig Gardens in the 1920's, and, below, the same house, now a private dwelling called Bishops Garth.*

date from about the same time as the Old Palace was begun, were of a simple timber house with a roof of red tiles. Its entrance opened onto the Palace grounds, and it was separated from South Street by a wooden fence. This building was soon replaced by a more substantial timber house, this time with foundation walls of flints from the beach.

From an examination of the rubbish the occupants left behind, we know that their diet included large amounts of oysters and other shellfish, as well as animal meats.

In the fifteenth century, later occupants of the house developed it further, and built a large hearth inside which seems to have been used for the manufacture of lead or pewter badges for pilgrims. During this period, the Palace seems to have been gradually surrounded by houses, including Parsonage Row (c1480), and the brewhouse (c1390). There is also evidence of further buildings to the east. By about 1530, however, the Palace had ceased to be used as such, and this house fell into disrepair and was eventually demolished. For the intervening three hundred years the site appears to have been used only as a garden.

The next house we come to is now called Bishops Garth. In its garden is one of the best known features of Tarring, a fig orchard. In the nineteenth century, the gardens were quite a tourist attraction, and were referred to in many early guide books. They were laid out with walks, and one of the trees carried a sign reading:

*This fig tree is the oldest in England*
*it was planted 800 years ago*
*by Thomas A Becket*

The suggestion that the trees were planted by St Thomas Becket himself is quite ridiculous, but it does seem that some of the present trees originate from cuttings of trees from the parsonage gardens in 1745.

Some older residents of the area with very long memories can recall walking across the fields from Worthing for cream teas in Miss Humphries' tea gardens, including, in the season, all the figs you could eat. The fig gardens were still open in 1936, but after the war, they were closed and the house became a private home with its present name.

A considerable portion of the garden was subsequently sold off and the trees grubbed up to make way for a new development, now known as Bishops Close. Further building is currently taking place in the garden, but it seems that some of the trees will be preserved. The extent of the original gardens can be gauged, since a section of the

*47. The old tree in the Fig Gardens, with a notice claiming it had been "planted by Thomas a'Becket -about AD 1162".*

original rear flint wall can still be seen at the end of Bishops Close.The house itself appears quite old, and there has been a dwelling on the site since at least 1631.

There is a legend that the beccafico, a small fig-eating bird of the warbler family, migrates each summer from Italy to Tarring for just one week to feast on the ripe figs. It is alleged that the bird is only ever seen in England in Tarring and Sompting, where there are also fig orchards, but I have not heard of a sighting in recent years or, indeed, at all.

South of this point, there is very little remaining evidence of old Tarring, although traces of history can be found. The area almost to the junction of Rectory Road was described in 1811 as old enclosed land, but appears to have been undeveloped. By 1839, however, there was a substantial farm here with extensive outbuildings. Soon afterwards, the farm building on the north of the site had been converted into a coachhouse which is now Flintstones, and one of the farm houses further developed into Norfolk House, then called The Elms. Elmslea looks to be considerably older, but was originally part of the fig garden tenement, perhaps a gardener's cottage.

The house at the junction of St Lawrence Avenue and South Street also seems to be old, but, in fact was probably built as late as 1880. Its older appearance derives from the skillful reuse of older materials, a practice which was well known in Tarring for many hundreds of years, and now, after a period during which it was out of favour, seems slowly to be returning, along with a growing interest in the conservation of old buildings.

St Lawrence Avenue comes next. In 1839, it did not exist, but by 1879, a track had been laid through from the street at this point to give access to the farmyard of the new West Tarring Farm, which stood under the St Lawrence surgery in Rectory Road. The farm had a short life, at least in Tarring terms, for by 1932 the farm buildings had been demolished to make way for Rectory Road, and the land sold for housing development, which by this time had a momentum which was to be halted only when all available land had been used up.

Moving south again, the northern section of the island of land contained by South Street, Rectory Road and St Lawrence Avenue was the site of Clarendon House, which was built in the 1840's as the farm house of West Tarring Farm. Confusingly, the house was originally called East Terring House. By 1875 it was a gentleman's residence, and survived the construction of the bypass, but it lost a large section of its rear garden to the road. It was only a matter of time before it, too, attracted the attention of the developers, and by the early 1960's, Tarring Gate stood in its place.

The southerly corner of Tarring Gate, a small block of flats, marks the site where the vicarage of Tarring stood for over three hundred years. In 1615, it was described [92] as *a dwelling house by ye selfe, and a small garden plott and orchard thereunto adjoining.* In common with many houses in Tarring, it was rebuilt at the end of the eighteenth century. In 1792, the vicar, Revd Edward Phillips, resided [93] *in a good home here built by his predecessor Sir Richard Ryecroft Bart of Penshurst Kent.* At the same time, Tarring, or rather Terring as it was called, was described as *Though...still but a small old town, its increase within these few years has been considerable.*

Since the ownership of the vicarage never changed, it was often used as a reference to describe the position of other houses in the court rolls. It became the rather grander rectory only in 1879, when the

*48. East Terring House in 1848, soon after it was built. It was the farmhouse of West Tarring Farm, and later, was called Clarendon House. Until it was demolished in 1960, it stood between South Street and Rectory Road, to the south of St Lawrence Avenue.*

incumbencies of vicar and rector were combined, but it is the latter name which has been perpetuated in Rectory Road, for which this house, too, made way in 1930. A new rectory was built to replace it farther up Rectory Road, on land which was part of the original parsonage glebe. Some of the original walls of the vicarage garden now surround the garden of number 12 Rectory Road, the house to the south of St Lawrence surgery.

To the south of the old vicarage garden was the start of the path to Heene, a twitten or narrow lane which was described in the early part of the century as a pleasant walk, through the centre of the market garden to Becket Road, along which in the spring could be seen masses of daffodils growing under the fruit trees. The twitten, as we have said, still exists, although the walk is not now so picturesque as it once was. The path followed briefly the northern pavement of

Haynes Road, before turning diagonally south along the northern pavement of Twitten Way.

*49. Clarendon House shortly before it was demolished in 1960, and, below, the new development which has replaced it.*

Immediately south of this path, in what is now the middle of Rectory Road, stood a lovely old thatched barn, the sort picture postcards are made of, but it too made way for the Tarring by-pass.

The house to which the barn belonged stood on the site of Kingdom Hall and was probably built, or rebuilt, in around 1610. It was known as Palmers. Having been constructed in the first major rebuilding of Tarring in the reign of Queen Elizabeth I, in 1816 it was caught up in the second great rebuilding of the late eighteenth and early nineteenth centuries, and was converted into three homes, and the barn sold off separately.

Sometime between 1839 and 1895, the most northerly section of the barn had been converted into a cottage known as the Haynes, or Haynes Cottage, presumably in memory of Love and Thomas Haynes, who lived in Palmers from 1745 to 1812 and, shortly before its demise, it was remembered as a sweet shop. Although the barn could not be preserved, the name is still commemorated in Haynes Road. The house itself was still three dwellings in 1895, and was demolished before 1932.

Snow Cottage, number 138 South Street, is altogether easier to date. It has a datestone showing the initials H.T. and the date 1881, and although such dates on buildings are notoriously unreliable, this one is confirmed by the first appearance of Snow Cottage in the Worthing directory for 1882. The initials probably refer to H. Tribe, who owned much of the land here and probably commissioned the building of the house. It was not built for his own use, however, since for the first five years of its existence it was occupied by Mr and Mrs Sheppard. The land on which the house was built had previously been a small, walled, orchard. In 1839, it was a garden owned by John Hide and earlier, in 1808, by William Margesson. From 1926 until after 1960, Snow Cottage was occupied by Percy Savary, a haulage contractor who owned the old Durrington Carriage Company.

The next three houses, in a terrace, were built around 1872, and were then called Park View. The name was appropriate at the time since there were only fields almost as far as the eye could see on the other side of the road. This situation did not last for long, though, as we shall see, and the houses eventually lost their original name, too.

*50. Haynes Cottage was another casualty of progress when Rectory Road was built. The wall on the left surrounded the vicarage garden, and the holm oak tree that grew there still stands today, as the bottom photograph shows.*

*51. Haynes Cottage from the south, and the same view, very much altered, today.*

The rest of the terrace, originally Morrison Villas, was added in around 1875. It was built as just two houses, but the centre section was converted into two more shops in the 1930's. It is interesting that in Victorian times, people avoided the name *cottage,* as a rather demeaning word for a small dwelling, whereas now it seems to hold great attraction. For example number 130 South Street, once number 1 Park View, is now called March Cottage, and its neighbour has become April Cottage.

52. *Another view of Haynes Cottage, taken in 1909, showing the wall of the vicarage garden on the left. The house on the right is Palmers, which stood on the site of the Kingdom Hall.*

The row of shops we reach next, called Park Buildings, was built in the early 1930's on the site of a small nursery with a cottage called Park Cottage. Yet another example of the preservation of an old name from the history of Tarring. The cottage was probably old, and could well have been the *cottage and garden adjacent in South Street* that stood about where the baker's shop is now, and belonged to John Hornesby in 1646. Even in 1921, close to three hundred years later, this cottage was still being described as *previously Hornby's.* A remarkable length of time for an ordinary working man to be remembered. The original nursery land at the rear of the site is now a builders yard.

The next, rather impressive block, was built in about 1895, and the southern house, number 102, has always been called Sunnyside. It was built on the site of a much smaller house which had stood here since at least 1648. The terrace was originally only two houses, and the splitting of number 104 into two is recent.

The site of number 100 is certainly old, and is one of the very few sites in the village not held as a copyhold tenancy. The present house probably retains at least some of the fabric of an earlier building, but had attained its present form by 1839. Mr W. Osborne Boyes, a solicitor, bought the house in 1893, renamed it Corndale, and built, as a folly in the garden, the flintstone tower which still stands there. It was designed as a study to give the solicitor an escape from his children, but has been disused for many years. It was restored in the 1950's, but has now started to decay again. At the time of writing, the house itself is being extensively restored, and it is to be hoped that this little idiosyncracy of nineteenth century Tarring will also now be looked after.

The area from here south to below Westland Avenue, now numbers 88 to 98 South Street, was a tenement held by George Hide in 1668 at a copyhold rent of 4d per annum. There was a house here then, which remained in 1811. Soon afterwards, the whole was converted, probably by major rebuilding, into four cottages. They must have been rather small, however, and by 1831 had been further altered into two larger ones.

Obadiah Chipper, a market gardener with land further down the street, probably lived here, at number 92, from when the cottages were built, and was succeeded by his son, who was still working here in 1905, when it was called Oak Cottage. Numbers 94 to 98 were the Victoria Tea Rooms at the turn of the present century, and later Victoria Cottage. The shops on the corner date from about 1930, when Westland Avenue was constructed.

ALFRED CARTER,

THE PEOPLE'S POPULAR CATERER

AND REFRESHMENT CONTRACTOR,

VICTORIA TEA GARDENS, WEST TARRING.

[RED FLAG.

*A.C. begs to inform Clergymen and Superintendents of Schools, Bands of Hope, and kindred Societies, that he is prepared to provide*

LUNCHEONS, DINNERS AND TEAS

AT WORTHING, LITTLEHAMPTON, OR BOGNOR,

*At moderate prices, on shortest notice.*

LARGE HALLS TO SEAT 200 TO 500 AT DINNER, OR 300 TO 800 AT TEA.

*Send for Testimonials and Tariff Price List.*

ON HIRE! MARQUEES of all sizes,—Plate,—Cutlery,—Linen, —Chairs,—Seats,—Decorations,—Tea and Coffee Urns,—China,—Glass, — Portable Coppers,—and Tabling,—at Moderate Charges.

WAITERS SUPPLIED.

ADDRESS:—

CARTER, Refreshment Contractor, West Tarring, Worthing, W.

MY MOTTO IS: Best Food, Plenty of it, and Efficient Waiting.

*53. The Victoria Tea Gardens, which flourished in the grounds of numbers 94 to 98 South Street for about ten years at the turn of the century. The contemporary advertisement is from the Parish Magazine.*

The site on the south corner of this junction marks the southern boundary of the old village of Tarring. It was for centuries the Church Pound, an enclosed field where animals found wandering in the village were taken, to be released only on payment of a fine. Hope Cottage was built on the front of this site, possibly in 1754, and was rebuilt and renamed, rather more prosaically, West View by Harold Baker, a haulage contractor who worked here from 1928 until 1956. The house was demolished in 1972 to make way for the garage which now occupies the site [94]. There had been a smaller filling station close by previously, from around 1930.

Below this point there were no further houses in 1870, just a road across the fields, which stretched right to the sea. Indeed, on the other side of the road, there were only two buildings south of Tarring Recreation Ground, and one of those was a barn.

The London, Brighton and South Coast Railway had been laid through the fields south of the village in 1846, but it was the opening of West Worthing station in the 1870's that was to have a dramatic effect on the appearance of the southern end of the village.

From this date onwards, a new conurbation began to grow outwards from the focus of the railway station. St Dunstans, Becket and Canterbury Roads, and the area south east of the station, were laid out almost at once, and the development grew ever northwards until it joined old Tarring. The effect on the village can be deduced from the population statistics.

In 1086, the earliest information we have shows 41 working men in the village, suggesting a population of perhaps 200; The 1641 Protestation return names 156 males over 18, indicating a population of about 500; and by 1881, over 200 years later, the census enumerated 733 inhabitants. But by 1901, just twenty years later, the population had more than doubled to 1720, and it has continued to grow rapidly thereafter.

The coming of the railway brought about major developments which were to change Tarring from a country village, and were to lead irrevocably to its absorption into Worthing, administratively partly in 1902 and finally in 1929, and physically on approximately the same timescale.

The two terraces nearest to the railway were originally known as

*54. West View, which occupied the site of West Tarring Filling Station in South Street, was demolished in 1972. The bottom photograph shows where it stood.*

Brighton and Hove Terraces, but no trace of these names remains. The more southerly, Brighton Terrace, was occupied entirely by gardeners in 1889, but traders slowly took over. Mr Sultun opened his butcher's shop on the north corner in about 1892, with his wares hanging in the open windows. By 1898 a confectioner, hairdresser, dining room, fishmonger, bootmaker and greengrocer had also been established. Subsequently, the shopping centre continued to develop northwards, although it has not quite joined up with the shops of old Tarring.

*55. Mr Sultun outside his butcher's shop at the turn of the century. The meat was displayed, unrefrigerated, in the open windows. Mrs Sultun kept the greengrocery shop next door.*

North of Brighton and Hove Terraces, number 46 was Clifton House, a name which can still just be discerned on the front wall, and number 38, which was called Windmill Cottage for no apparent reason, still has a small sign to this effect. Architecturally, this section of the street has suffered from unco-ordinated piecemeal alterations which have all but destroyed the original unity of the development. However, with close inspection and some imagination it is possible to picture the scene at the turn of the century.

The crossroads which now lies south of the railway is old, and used to be called the south cross of Tarring, or Tarring Cross. Until late in the last century it was a T-junction, with the road to the left leading to Broadwater Lane, and on the right, to the path to the sea and Goring Cross.

*56. South Street as it looked about eighty years ago, and the same view today.*

Crossing the road, we move rapidly north along the west side of South Street, finding little of real historic interest along the way. The shops between St Dunstans and Canterbury Roads were built originally as a terrace of houses with small front gardens, but these were lost when South Street was widened. A Baptist church was first built on the north corner of Canterbury Road in 1901, although the present building dates from 1938.

*57. These shops on the west side of South Street were originally built as private houses, as the left hand photograph shows. They were converted in the 1930's, when their front gardens made way for the widening of the road.*

At the junction with Ethelred Road was a croft of land called Brunes in 1610 and still in 1843. By then, a small cottage had been erected on the site, but it was short-lived, and in less than a hundred years had made way for modern Tarring.

The field where Athelstan and Ethelwulf Roads now stand was half of an ancient yardland called Braziers, and the site of Parkfield Road was called Stormes or Stonecroft, leading back as far as what is now

Church Road. On the north corner were three small cottages in 1839, but they had gone by 1912. This may also have been the site of a slaughterhouse mentioned between 1895 and 1903. A local resident remembered fairs being held in these fields in the summer [95], a particular attraction being the Tarring Derby, held during the Tarring Flower Show in August. The race took place over two laps of the field, between Ambrose Chipper, in full jockey dress, riding the horse which was more used to pulling his baker's cart, and Mr Jordan the coal merchant, riding his cart-horse.

In 1893, there was a serious epidemic of typhoid fever in Worthing [96], and the inhabitants of the new houses in this part of Tarring were badly affected. The outbreak began when the water supply of the town became contaminated with sewage. Everyone was warned to boil all drinking water, and eventually the number of new cases abated, but not before 284 people had succumbed to the fever, of whom 38 had died. The tourist trade was at this time vital to the local economy of Worthing, and the outbreak had caused considerable concern among prospective visitors. As a result, the officers of the town were anxious to declare that the epidemic was over, and on June 14th, after no new cases had been reported for some time, they did so.

This was a tragic error, since people immediately stopped the boiling of drinking water which was still contaminated, and two weeks later, the disease returned. The second phase of the epidemic was a full-scale disaster. Those residents who could, packed up and left the town altogether, and there were no summer visitors, since the outbreak was by now being reported in the national press.

Fresh water was supplied from tanks in the streets, while the search continued for the source of the contamination. Not until September was the water supply returned to purity, by which time 1261 people in Worthing alone, one in every twelve of the population, had fallen victim to the fever, and 155 had died.

During the second outbreak, there were 55 cases of typhoid recorded in Tarring, mostly in the new streets in this area, and there were nine deaths. The hospital in Worthing was in no position to cope with these cases, so the Old Palace, then in use as an infants' school, and the newly built Parish Reading Room nearby, were pressed into service as temporary hospitals.

In order to avoid a recurrence of the tragedy, the old shallow wells in High Street, Worthing were replaced by a new pumping station in Broadwater [97], opened in 1897, and this was supplemented by a further pumping station at Patching in 1927. Water from Patching was delivered to the reservoir at Durrington, from which Tarring still receives its water today.

At the junction of South Street and Rectory Road is the entrance to The Priory. It has never been a priory, nor does it have any religious connections. It was built as a private house in about 1880 on the site of an old barn, and was originally called Parkfield. By 1900, it had acquired its present name, and became first a residential hotel, and then an old peoples' home, between the wars. The grounds of the house originally reached to the street, and to the recreation ground in the north, but the land fronting South Street was sold off in the early 1930's for the further development which stands here today.

The Tarring Recreation Ground is an old tenement of enclosed land called Taints. A barn stood on the northern corner adjacent to the street in 1668, and remained there for two hundred years, but had disappeared by 1880. The ancient footpath across this field originally began in the centre of the frontage, rather than the northern corner, and ran diagonally across the field to an old orchard in the grounds of what was then Church House.

The line of the path was changed in the early part of the present century, probably in 1923 when the field was acquired by the Borough Council for use as a recreation ground, but the site of the original entrance can still be identified both from a gap in the low edging wall that borders South Street, and the remains of the original path inside the grounds at this point.

Meadowbank, although itself a relatively modern house, marks our return from nineteenth century developments to the site of old Tarring proper. There was a *Mansion House called Peeters* here in 1610. It was occupied, together with a barn in High Street, by Thomas South when he died in 1651, and was subsequently granted to his wife Elizabeth for her widow's bench. The record of the death of Thomas is the first entry in the roll in English, and is reproduced here to give the reader some flavour of the language used. The words used were little different in the final entries in the rolls in the 1930's:

| | | |
|---|---|---|
| TARRINGE | The Courte of William Garway esquire Lord of the said Manor there holden the five and twentieth day of September 1651 By Edward Raynes gent Steward there | |
| Bayliffe | William Fletcher bayliffe there appeared | |
| The homage | Michael Wheatley<br>William Wheatley<br>Robert Porchester<br>John Parson<br>Thomas Hamper<br>William Warrell sen<br>William Warrell iun<br>Thomas Warrell sen<br>Thomas Warrell iun | John Hornesbie<br>John Leech<br>Edward Tourle(?)<br>Richard Weston<br>John Beale in<br>right of his wife<br>William Hamper<br>Philip Capon |

The death of Thomas Southe — At this courte it is presented by homage that Thomas Southe which held of the Lord of this Manor as of this Manor to him and his heirs by copy of Courtroll at the will of the Lord according to the custome of the said Manor A House and a garden in the Southstreet of Tarringe and a crofte of land to the same adjoining and belonging contayning by estimation an acre late Hendries and paying to the Lord yearly iiiid lately died thereof seised After whose death happened to the lord for a heriot xs of certaine And that James Southe his youngest sonne and according to the custome of this Manor next heire and of full age And that Elizabeth South widow is his relict and ought by the custome this manor to hold the premises as her widowes bench according to the custome of this Manor that is to say so long as shee shall live sole chast and unmarried who present in Courte praies to bee thereunto admitted To whom the Lord by his Steward aforesaid granted thereof seisin by the rodd To have & to hold to said Elizabeth and her assignes as her widowes bench according to the custome of the Manor aforesaid by the rents customes and other service therefore first due and of right accustomed And she is admitted tenant in form aforesaid gives to the Lord for A fine iiiid that is to say as much as the premises pay to the Lord yearly And she did therefore fealtie.

heriot xs of certaine

fine - iiiid

Within a year, however, Elizabeth was forced to forfeit her widow's bench, and give up the house to her son James *for having lately taken to husband one Thomas Botting*. Since the said Thomas was one of the most substantial property owners in the village at the time, however, it would have been no real hardship. The present house was built on the site of the earlier property in around 1893, for a Doctor Hubert.

There has been a house on the site of Pendules for many years, though the present house dates from the beginning of the ninteenth century. In 1654 a cottage here was owned by Margaret Beale, the daughter of William Selden, and possibly the sister of John Selden. In 1793 it passed to William Tribe, but was almost certainly let, since the Tribes held one of the smith's shops in High Street. The house, and the adjacent barn, were most likely thatched, and in 1803, disaster struck.

A graphic account of the tragedy was given in the local paper [98]:

*About noon on Wednesday last, a dreadful fire broke out at West Tarring in this county, which in a very short space of time, so rapid was its progress, reduced to ashes seven dwelling houses (three of which were in two tenements), and nearly all the furniture, wearing apparel, and other property which they contained, three barns with a quantity of unthreashed wheat, and 15 loads of straw, two stables, a woodhouse, carthouse, two wagons, three carts, and divers impliments of husbandry. The damage altogether, is estimated at upwards of two thousand pounds, and nearly the whole of the property was uninsured. Fifty-one persons, most of them helpless women and children, are reduced to the utmost distress by this melancholy accident and have no other means of replacing their loss than by the liberal contributions by a humane and generous public. The widow Pullen, whose loss is estimated at £400, appears to be the greatest sufferer. The fire was occasioned by the carelessness of a man employed in baking, who after heating his oven threw the hot coals into an ash-hole amongst some shavings and furze, which soon burst into a flame and communicated to the houses.*

The site of the fire was broadly the area from the present shoe repair shop almost to the entrance to Priory Close. It is interesting to note that this relatively small piece of land contained 10 separate homes housing fifty-one people.

In 1804, when Thomas Loud bought the tenement, it is described as a dwelling house recently destroyed by fire, but in 1824, reference is made to a new dwelling erected by Thomas Loud.

The fire was certainly remembered long after the event, and every subsequent transfer refers to it. Even the last entry, recording the granting of the freehold to Fred Cheesman in 1920 includes the description:

*All that piece and parcel of ground whereon a dwelling house was formerly destroyed by fire on which a messuage and dwelling house with outbuildings has since been erected and built and now known as Pendules.*

Later in the nineteenth century, what is now the little shoe repair shop to the south was the village fire station, where the hand-drawn cart was kept. By 1890, water was being supplied to the village by the West Worthing Waterworks Company, which must have greatly improved the villagers' ability to fight fires. The West Tarring Fire Brigade Station remained here in 1921, at which time Mr Carr, a shoemaker, lived in Pendules. Presumably, sometime not long after this, the building was converted to its present use.

Following the fire, a new house was built on what is now the southern corner of the junction with Priory Close. It was owned from 1841 until 1922 by Alexander Ramsay, and when he died its new owner called it Ramsay Cottage. This house too was demolished in around 1938 when Priory Close was built.

If you look at the present day map of Tarring, you will see that the site of the houses in Priory Close, together with the two houses in South Street on either side of the entrance, occupy a piece of land which could be described as toadstool shaped, with the base of the toadstool in South Street. This would suggest that the development was built on a piece of land carved out from earlier, larger, sites, but here that is not the case, and this tenement seems to have been this shape for many centuries.

In 1650 it was a tenement, described as being in the market-place of Tarring, containing a building called the stone-healed house, owned by William Hamper. Healed means roofed, and so the name signified that the house was roofed with Horsham stone slabs, as the Parsonage Row cottages are today. Also on the site were two barns, a malthouse, orchards and gardens, although by 1773, when the tenement passed into the hands of the Pelling family, the barns were being used as stables.

The property was usually let during this period, and in 1806 was partly owned by Francis Pelling, who was a private in His Majesty's Fourth Regiment of Royal Irish Dragoon Guards. As such, he could well have been fighting in the war with France which was raging at the time. He evidently survived, however, and sold his share to his brother Hugh in 1814.

Mr H. Hills lived in the stone-healed house from about 1896 until it was demolished in the early 1930's, to make way for the new Priory Close. The north wall of the tenement can still be seen, however, and some older residents may remember it. For a short period during the thirties stood, north of here, the West Tarring Bedding and Upholstery Works, owned by H. Muggeridge and A. Richardson.

CHAPTER NINE

# THE SHIP

The large building on the south of the market-place, from the greengrocer to the baker, has been associated with shops since as early as 1610. Edward Weston owned two shops and Robert Houlden another here then, and by 1642, all three had been bought by Thomas Botting. In 1658, when Thomas died, the tenement was described as *all that Market House now lately built in the town of Tarring,* and was further precisely identified with the earlier shops.

Presumably the building which was new in 1658 housed the Tarring corn market, which was held weekly on Saturdays, and was one of the most important markets in the county. Its origins go back to 1444, when the area was under regular threat from foreign raiding parties. The villagers of Tarring were suffering, as they describe in their petition to King Henry VI [99]:

> *Your humble oraturs the men of the town of Terring in the shyre of Sussex, upon the sea banks dwelling, that where they often tymes by the Kynges enemys of Ffraunce, Breteygne* (Brittany), *Spayne, and other partys, thereby the se costes a werre farre passynge many and grete harmes and losses in thaire bodys and in thaire godes hav suffret, and yet continually sufferen, so that for asmoche as the sayd town hath hadd no market the men ther beyng atte the next market, they that were abyding and beleyving in the said town stille in the mene while by the said enemys hav dyvers tymis ben taken prisoners and byn slayn as well the men as the women, childer, maidenes, wives and doters therein beying and beleyving.*

It is possible of course that there is some element of exaggeration in the description. A corn market would have been an important contributor to the local economy, and the petition certainly pleads an eloquent case. The honesty of the petitioners must surely be questioned when we realise that the next market [100] was at Broadwater!

A charter was nevertheless duly granted [101] by King Henry VI on June 11th 1444:

*Henry, by the grace of God King of England and France and Lord of Ireland, to the Archbishops, Bishops, Abbots, Priors, Dukes, Marquises, Earls, Viscounts, Mayors, Bailiffs, Constables, Attendants, and all faithful people to whom these presents shall come, greeting: Know ye that whereas we are informed in the humble petition of our beloved subjects, the men dwelling in the village of Tarring, in the county of Sussex, situate near the sea, that they at various times do sustain and suffer great injury both in their persons and goods from our enemies of France, and from other parts; because, as they say, having no Market of their own, during their absence at the next Market they are in terror lest their village should be ransacked and their goods taken. We have taken their request into consideration, and desirous to alleviate and support our subjects in this part of the realm, as we are bound to do, have, as a special favour for ourselves and our heirs, as much as in us lies, granted to the men dwelling in the said village of Tarring, to have, and to hold for ever, a Market for themselves and their successors every week, to be holden at the aforesaid village of Tarring on Saturday, provided it does not interfere with any other neighbouring market. Witnesses the Venerable Father, John Stafford, Archbishop of Canterbury, Primate of all England, our Chancellor; William Alnwick, Bishop of Lincoln; Thomas Beckington, Bishop of Bath and Wells; and William Strickland, Bishop of Carlisle; our dearly beloved Uncle, Humphrey, Duke of Gloucester; our dearly beloved Cousin, Humphrey Stafford, Earl of Devon; and William de la Pole, Earl of Suffolk, our House Steward; also our beloved and faithful Ralph, Lord Cromwell, our Treasurer; and Ralph Botteler, Knight and Master Adam Molyneux, Keeper of our Privy Seal, and others. Dated at Westminster the 11th day of June in the 22nd year of our reign.*

*Southe, by Writ of Privy Seal and of the date aforesaid, by authority of Parliament.*

The market continued to be held here on Saturdays [102], originally for corn, but subsequently for other goods, including apparently livestock and other agricultural products, until at least 1821. The building of the Market Hall shows how important the market had become by 1650.

*58. The market-place, with the Market House on the right, and the Parish Reading Room on the left.*

There is a record [103], in around 1540, of a complaint by Richard Brode of Rusper, who sent a lad to buy three bushels of wheat from Tarring market to make bread. As the lad was riding home through Findon, John Michelborne, one of the bailiffs of the sheriff of Sussex, stopped him and confiscated the wheat. The result of the complaint is not recorded, but it is interesting to note that a common citizen had the right of complaint to the King about the matter. The fact that Richard thought it worthwhile to send a lad all the way from Rusper is another indication of how important the Tarring market was in those days.

Tarring was the most important town in the area in the eighteenth century. The 1798 directory lists Tarring as a market town, but refers to Goreing, Ferring, Patching, Clapham, Findon, Sompting, Broadwater and Heene, erroneously called Steen, as nearby villages. The same guidebook contains a description of Worthing, again as a village near Tarring, which is interesting as showing the very beginnings of the development of the modern seaside resort:

*Worthing, in the parish of Broadwater, two miles distant. This village is close by the sea, and is now much frequented in the summer season by people of fashion for bathing, on account of the fine sands, which are esteemed the best in the kingdom. A fishery is carried on here in the spring for mackerel, and in the fall for herrings. It has a fair on July 20, 21, and 22. - Here is an elegant seat belonging to the Right Hon. the Earl of Warwick; and many good houses for lodgings finished, and some building. It has likewise three good inns, viz. Seahorse, New Inn, and Anchor, for the accomodation of strangers.*

In addition to the weekly market, Tarring has long had two annual fairs. These date back even further than the market, one existing in 1348, and the other having been originally granted by charter of King Edward II to the Archbishop of Canterbury in 1314 for St Andrews Eve (September 21st). By 1798 it was being held eleven days later, on October 2nd, probably reflecting the change from the Julian to the Gregorian calendar in 1752.

In order to bring the British calendar into line with that which had been in use for many years in most of continental Europe, the Calendar (New Style) Act of 1750 decreed that the day following September 2nd 1752 would be September 14th. This caused widespread dissent, because many people thought that they were actually losing eleven days of their lives. Some things never change, however. The tax year ended previously on March 25th, a quarter day, but rather than lose eleven days revenue, the Inland Revenue simply changed the end of the tax year to eleven days later, thus explaining the rather curious date of April 5th which survives to this day.

In around 1778 the old Market House was demolished, and was replaced by the present building. It has been suggested that the original Market House was further up the street towards the church, and Sayers [104] provides a detailed exposition both of its location and its destruction. However his account provides no references, and since his writings show provable inaccuracies in other areas, it seems probable that the Market House was always on this site. Certainly the manor court records provide an unbroken series of transactions in a tenement called the Market House here in 1658 and Fenner's grocery shop which undoubtedly occupied the present building in 1910.

**VICTORIA TEA GARDENS,**
**WEST TARRING, Worthing.**

SCHOOL, GARDEN, AND OTHER PARTIES PROVIDED FOR, LARGE OR SMALL.
MARQUEES of all Sizes, ON HIRE.
LUNCHEON, DINNER, and TEA, on SHORTEST NOTICE.
ALFRED CARTER, CATERER, PROPRIETOR.

*Repairs promptly executed.*
WINDOW BLINDS OF EVERY DESCRIPTION MADE AND REPAIRED
CARPENTERING. JOINERING.
**HORACE MITCHELL,**
Builder, Decorator, and Furnishing Undertaker.
**Myrtle Cottage, West Tarring**
Orders by Post punctually attended to.
ESTIMATES PROVIDED FOR ANY DESCRIPTION OF WORK

**HIGHFIELD FARM DAIRY COMPANY,**
ESTABLISHED 1866.
PURE FRESH MILK SUPPLIED MORNING AND AFTERNOON FROM GRASS-FED COWS.
HEAD OFFICE—23, NEW STREET, WORTHING
Branches—WORDSWORTH ROAD. 131, CLIFTON ROAD.
The milk supplied from the Company's Dairy Farms at West Tarring, Salvington and Broadwater.

**A. S. CHIPPER,**
Home - Made Bread Baker,
GROCER,
COAL — AND — WOOD — MERCHANT,
WEST TARRING.

Finest Quality of Groceries & Provisions. Finest Brands of BACON.
**G. FENNER,**
**Market House, WEST TARRING,**
And Down View Stores, WEST WORTHING.
Grocer, Tea Dealer & Provision Merchant,
DRAPER AND OUTFITTER.
*Boots and Shoes. Ironmongery and Earthenware. Agent W. & A. Gilbey's Wines and Spirits. Stone's British Wines. Mazawattee Tea.*
AGENT NORTH BRITISH AND MERCANTILE FIRE AND LIFE INSURANCE COMPANY.

**ALBURY,**
Church Road, Tarring.
CLASS FOR DAY PUPILS from 5 to 15 years.
MODERATE TERMS.
Piano Lessons to beginners.

**GEO. STANDING & SONS,**
Plumber & Gasfitter, General Builder Painter, Glazier, Paperhanger, & House Decorator
Drains and Sanitary work. Hot and Cold Water Fitter. Repairs in all Branches
ORDERS BY POST PUNCTUALLY ATTENDED TO.
Agent Norwich Union and Union Assurance Societies.
**2, GORDON TERRACE, WEST TARRING.**
CARPETS taken up, Beaten and Re-laid.
Close to West Worthing Station.

**F. F. MARSHALL**
WHOLESALE and RETAIL
Confectioner & Tobacconist.
NEWSAGENT.
Finest Brands of Cigars and Cigarettes.
Gentlemen's
Haircutting & Shaving Saloon.
Razors Ground and Set.
TARRING CROSSING.

**G. DUFFIELD,**
**Builder, Contractor, and Decorator,**
**CRANBOURNE VILLA, WEST TARRING.**
Furnishing Undertaker

**E. C. CORPS & SON**
Specialities: Poultry Foods. Pigeon ,, Parrot ,, Cage Bird ,, S.R. Flour ,, Garden Seed. Superfine Lawn Grass Seeds.
South St., WEST TARRING

IVOR HOUSE, TARRING ROAD
(Opposite West Worthing Station).
**GEO. W. WEST,**
GENERAL & FANCY DRAPER,
MILLINER AND DRESSMAKER.
High Class Dressmaking. Perfect Fit and Style guaranteed.

**SAMUEL CLARK,**
Practical Saddler & Harness Maker,
Clifton House, South Street, West Tarring.
All kinds of Harness and Saddlery bought and sold on commission. Any Article in the Trade made or obtained. Portmanteaus and Travelling Bags repaired. Estimates Free.

**T. STEVENS,**
PRACTICAL BOOT & SHOE MAKER.
SPECIAL ATTENTION TO REPAIRS.
FAMILIES & SCHOOLS WAITED UPON.
TERMS MODERATE.
1, BRIGHTON TERRACE,
WEST TARRING.

*59. These advertisements appeared in the parish magazine at different times in the early years of this century.*

*60. Cottages to the south east of Market House being demolished in 1966. As the lower photograph shows, the site has not yet been redeveloped.*

Fenner's was established here by 1872, and continued in business until just before the first war. The shop was then occupied by Hales the baker, and was also the post and telegraph office until the thirties, when it became Roberts the wine merchant, and the post office was transferred back to the High Street. The three properties that currently make up this block are still called Market Buildings.

As well as the cottage on the south side of the building, now a greengrocery, there was originally a further cottage to the south which was demolished in 1966.

Moving on towards the church, the next three cottages were built in the early years of the nineteenth century, and are thus contemporary with a number of other houses in the village. They replaced an older, single house which had stood here since at least 1638, when it was owned by Francis Brian. He also owned the George, or the White Horse as it was then, across the street, and it seems possible that the two sites were originally a single tenement, with a narrow lane through the middle leading to the church.

Continuing past these three cottages, we find little evidence of old Tarring until we reach the church. However, there was a timber-framed house, known as The Old Cottage, on the land immediately adjacent, now numbers 50 to 52 Church Road, until it was demolished after the war. Given its apparent age, it was almost certainly the old cottage called Ashers which stood here in 1610.

In 1673, it was described as being in the Church Lane also West Lane, the first reference to either of these street names for what is now Church Road. A gate to the east of the cottage gave access to a barn at the rear, which may survive, much altered, in the complex of old farm buildings which are now reached by way of the lane at the side of the church.

*61. The south side of Church Road, showing the old cottage called Ashers which stood here until after the war. The lower photograph shows the same scene today.*

*62. The Old Cottage from the west, in a state of considerable disrepair, and the site as it is today.*

To the west of The Old Cottage, on the site of the maisonettes numbered 42 to 48, was a tenement which in 1643 was called the Ship. It was almost certainly an inn, although as such it was relatively short lived. We know that the White Horse was the only inn in 1636, and although the Ship was still so called in 1650, by 1678 and subsequently it was only referred to as a messuage. In 1839 it had been converted into no less than five separate dwellings, and remained so until it was demolished in 1888.

*63. The Old Cottage in Church Road before it was allowed to decay.*

These were the last houses fronting the road and the land to the west was part of the demesne of the manor. The site of the present Church House was, by the end of the eighteenth century, occupied by an impressive manor house, with a substantial garden. The house had three storeys, unusual for Tarring, with dormer windows and a Horsham stone roof. Almost certainly, manor courts were held here, and the gate into the front garden was called the Court Gate.

The house was the farmhouse of Church Farm, the demesne farm, and was occupied in the early nineteenth century by perhaps Tarring's most famous resident, Thomas Henty [105]. The farm was a mixed farm, and as well as growing the usual crops, Henty raised stock, and in particular bred sheep. At the time his flock consisted entirely of merino sheep, a breed which had been brought to England some years earlier by George III to improve the quality of English wool.

*64. This watercolour, painted in 1888, shows The Old Cottage, and the tenement called the Ship which originally stood to the west of it. The lower photograph shows how different Church Road looks now.*

In 1829, induced by the offer of a large grant of land, he sent his three eldest sons to Australia. They sailed from Littlehampton in a ship with 150 pure-bred merino sheep and other stock, and over thirty men and women from Tarring. They went first to Western Australia, but soon moved to Tasmania.

Despite the enormous difficulties of communication over such vast distances, they must have managed to send back good reports of conditions there because in 1831, Thomas Henty himself sold up all of his farming stock and equipment, and set sail with the rest of his family to join his sons.

*65. This imposing house near the church was the home of the Henty family before they emigrated to Australia in 1829. The house is seen looking south from Church Road. It was demolished towards the end of the nineteenth century, although the front garden wall can still be recognized.*

The Hentys prospered in Australia. In 1834, Edward, Thomas's sixth son, landed at Portland Bay, and established the first permanent settlement in what is now the State of Victoria. Moving inland, he established extensive sheep-runs, and continued to improve the quality of his flock. His work, and that of his brothers, some of whom joined him later, made a significant contribution to the successful development of the sheep farming industry in Australia.

*66. A drawing of the church in 1825, showing the house where the Hentys lived on the right, and farm buildings in front of the church. The artist was sitting in the centre of the field called The Taints, now the Tarring Recreation Ground.*

The Hentys' house had been demolished by 1898, and in its place a two-storied classic Victorian house, known as Church House, was built. Later, when the farm lands had been given over to housing development, the house was known as Tarring Court, reflecting its ancient association with the manor, but it too was demolished in 1964. It was replaced by a small development of sheltered accomodation which also preserves a connection with the past through its name, Church House.

Excavations which were carried out during the rebuilding showed that the site has a very long history [106]. Evidence of occupation dating back to the twelfth century was discovered, together with a mid-eighteenth century icehouse, an underground storage place for perishable foods in the days before refrigeration.

*67. The left hand photograph shows Church House, the Victorian building which replaced the Hentys' house. It was demolished in 1964, but the sheltered housing development which replaced it bears the same name. On the right is the new building from the same viewpoint.*

CHAPTER TEN

# CHURCH ALES

We now come to the church itself. The oldest parts of the building date from the thirteenth century, the same period in which the Old Palace was constructed, but the history of the Church in this area goes back much further.

In the year 678, a dispute arose between King Egfrid and Wilfred, later Saint Wilfred, who was Bishop of Northumbria. As a result, Wilfred left the diocese, and travelled to Rome. On his return, he was unable to return to Northumbria, and so instead he came to Sussex to preach the gospel to the pagan South Saxons. There was a small and poor monastery at Bosham, and it was from here that Wilfred commenced his ministry, with immediate and startling results, as the monk Bede related [107]:

*No rain had fallen in the province for three years prior to his arrival, and a terrible famine had ensued, which reduced many to an aweful death. It is said that frequently forty or fifty emaciated and starving people would go to a precipice, or to the edge of the sea, where they would join hands and leap over, to die by the fall or by drowning. But on the very day that the nation received the baptism of faith a soft but ample rainfall refreshed the earth, restoring greenness to the cornfields and giving a happy and fruitful season.*

And that was not all. Bede continued:

*When Wilfred had first arrived in the province and found so much misery from famine, he taught the people to obtain food by fishing; for although fish were plentiful in the sea and rivers, the people had no knowledge of fishing and caught only eels. So the bishop's men collected eel-nets from all sides and cast them into the sea, where, by the aid of God's grace, they quickly caught three hundred fishes of various kinds. These they divided into three portions, giving a hundred to the poor, a hundred to those who had lent their nets, and retaining a hundred for their own needs.*

As a result of these spectacular events, and Wilfred's enthusiasm, Christianity spread rapidly in Sussex. In 762, the King granted land in Ferring for the building of a monastery [108], and further woodland was granted [109] in 791.

By 941, as we have seen, Tarring was given to the Archbishop of Canterbury. With few written records, memories were short, and by 1086, Tarring had *always been in the hands of the monastery* [110]. We know [111] that there were monks here by 1189, and it is possible that a monastery of Tarring existed at the time of the Domesday survey. There was certainly a church here by then, although probably only a wooden structure.

In about the year 1175, there was a chaplain of the church in Tarring called William [112]. He was in dispute with the abbot of the priory at Sele, in Bramber, over the ownership of the tithes of Durrington. The Archbishop of Canterbury eventually reconciled the two parties, who agreed jointly to build a barn in the cemetery of Durrington, each holding a key, and to share the tithes equally between them.

*68. The church and the village pond at the turn of the century.*

Major parts of the present church were standing by the middle of the thirteenth century, when Simon of Tarring was the rector. In 1244, the Bishop of Chichester died, and the canons of the cathedral choose his successor [113]. Their nominee, Robert Passlew, was apparently a very objectionable man, but much in favour with King Henry III. The Archbishop of Canterbury overruled this choice, and appointed instead Richard of Wyche, who, following periods of study at Oxford Bologna and Orleans, had become his chancellor at Canterbury.

The King was enraged, and complained to the Pope, but Richard's cause prevailed, and the Pope confirmed his appointment. At this, the King seized the Bishop's Palace at Chichester, and forbade anyone to give Richard shelter or lend him money. Richard appealed in person to the King, but was met with a torrent of abuse. Since his palace was barred to him, he turned to his old friend Simon of Tarring, and from this refuge he travelled Sussex as a roving priest. It is during his stay here that he is supposed to have grafted a bud onto a barren fig tree, and started the association of Tarring with figs which has lasted to the present day.

Eventually, after the Pope had threatened Henry with excommunication, the King gave way, and Richard was restored to his rightful position. Richard died in 1253. The story of his life is liberally scattered with miraculous tales, including one occasion in Ferring when he fed 3000 people with bread estimated to be sufficient only for 90, and in 1262 he was canonized as Saint Richard of Chichester. His tomb in the cathedral subsequently became a popular place of pilgrimage, until it was destroyed in 1538 by the King's commissioners.

During this period and earlier, the right of sanctuary was in regular use in Tarring church. Dating back to King Ethelbert [114] in the year 597, it provided a temporary refuge for criminals on the run. Any fugative from justice who was able to reach the church or the churchyard was allowed to remain there for up to forty days. During this time he was allowed to avoid trial by admitting his crime before a coroner. He was then given free passage to a seaport to leave the country. The last record of abjuration, or taking an oath of voluntary exile, in Sussex [115] was in 1533.

The procedure is described [116] in a custumal for Winchelsea:

*If a man flee to Holy Church the Mayor as Coroner shall visit him to question him as to the cause of his flight, and if he formally acknowledges committing a felony he shall lose all his goods and chattels as forfeits, for which the Bailiff shall answer to the King. He shall live in the Church for forty days if he wishes and choose the Port from which he shall depart, and if he abjures within forty days it shall be accepted. After his abjuration he shall take his Cross and the Mayor shall proclaim in the King's name that no one on pain of forfeiture of life and limb shall do him harm or molest him, provided that he keeps on the road to the above mentioned Port.*

In 1249, John le Messier took sanctuary in Tarring church after stabbing Simon de Goringes with a knife [117]. However, he escaped before he could be deported, and the village was fined for allowing it to happen. Again in 1360, John Skyr *slew Richard atte Hale in West Tarring in self-defence*. John fled to Tarring church, but was ultimately acquitted [118].

There are not many such recorded instances of violent crime in Tarring, but a particularly full report of one is found in the records of the Sussex coroner [119] for June 30th 1517:

*On 28 June, when Robert Burne late of West Tarring, husbondman, was in the house of Edward Hamper...at West Tarring, John Tomson, vicar of West Tarring, and Martin, his servant, came and murdered him. Tomson struck him to the heart with a knife worth 1d which he held in his right hand and Martin struck him in the stomach with a dagger worth 8d which he held in his right hand, together giving him wounds of which he immediately died. On the same day John Watkynson late of West Tarring, chaplain, supported, comforted and abetted them, knowing that they had committed the murder.*

Tomson and Watkynson had fled, but the jury found them guilty in their absence, and they were outlawed. There is no record of them ever having been caught. Quite what Robert Burne had done to warrant being murdered by the vicar is, unfortunately, not recorded.

In 1561, an inventory [120] was made of the church's few possessions in accordance with an instruction of Queen Elizabeth I:

*A cope of red silk and two vestments, one of white damask and another of green silk. A banner of silk and a streamer of blue bokeram. Two banners, two pieces of stained cloth for the communion table and a canopy of old velvet. A mass book, a manual, two antiphoners and one prescenter. Two large and two small candlesticks in brass, and brass pots for water. A pair of censors, a crysmatory of tin, a little box of brass and a brass cross with a foot. An iron hammer and two lead pulls, with some iron, for the clock. A brass pyx, a foot for the cross and another pyx.*

The whole inventory was valued at £6.67, although of course it was then stated in the old currency as £6 13s 4d.

69. *A drawing of the church from the west, dating from before 1853.*

While this church furniture may seem familiar to present day churchgoers, the way it was used would have been less so [121]. There was no altar as such in the Elizabethan church. Instead, the congregation sat or stood around a wooden altar table in the body of the church, and it was from here that communion was dispensed. There would have been a large congregation for these services, since attendance was compulsory by law. Later, when attendance became voluntary, congregations declined, and William Cobbett, writing of one of his rural rides through Kent in 1823, said:

*It is very true, that the labouring people have, in a great measure, ceased to go to Church. There were scarcely any of that class at this great country church today... I can remember when they were so numerous, that the parson could not attempt to begin, till the rattling of their nailed shoes ceased.*

In the fifteenth and sixteenth centuries, the church was treated with much less reverence than today, and the nave acted as a sort of church hall. In particular, it was the scene of regular "church ales", at which the churchwardens sold ale in the church to raise funds. By all accounts, these were riotous occasions, and the churchwardens accounts make regular reference to them [122].

The first record is of one on Trinity Sunday, 1515, and they continued to be held regularly over the next fifty years. A problem arose in 1550, however, when a loss of 8s 6d was made - not at all the object of the exercise! The lesson was clearly learnt, and by 1561, the scale of the venture had been considerably increased. In that year, the churchwardens bought, among other things, a leg and half a carcase of mutton, two calfs' heads, twelve loaves of bread, vinegar, saffron, and of course a considerable quantity of hops and malt. In addition, they paid wages to a cook, a bagpipe player and some minstrels, and bought bells for the morris dancers.

This larger venture proved a financial success, with and outlay of almost £6 producing receipts of over £11, and another church ale was held in Heene in the same year. By 1566, the churchwardens could even afford to pay for the services of a dishwasher. Church ales were by this time being discouraged by both Church and State, and the last record of one being held in Tarring occurs in 1589.

Although the Elizabethan congregation used the prayer book we still know today, the psalms were sung rather than said or chanted, and prayers were never intoned. The psalms were sung from the metrical psalter of Sternhold and Hopkins, which contained rhymed versions of all the psalms. A few such metrical psalms still appear in modern hymn books, the best known of which is the hymn "All People that on Earth do Dwell", to the tune Old Hundredth. It is, of course the metrical version of psalm 100.

These psalms were sung to the accompaniment of an organ, which was used in the church [123] as early as 1570. Music has continued to play a part in the life of the church ever since. At times there have been church bands, and in the nineteenth century [124], the band which accompanied the singing comprised James Newman, George and James Chipper, clarionets; Thomas Binstead, bass viol; Charles Bushby, trombone; Charles and Thomas Chipper, bassoons.

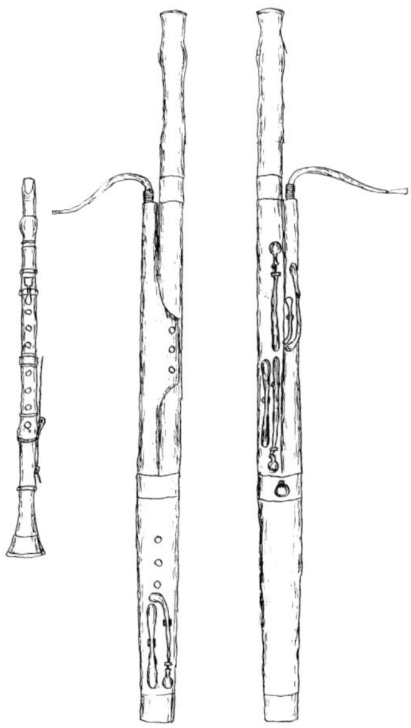

*70. A clarinet and two bassoons which were used in the church band in the nineteenth century.*

Edward Sayers, a solicitor's clerk who lived for some years at The Hollies in High Street, and took a keen interest in local history, wrote [125] of his early years in the 1850's:

> *Some of the choir formed a choral class, for the purpose of learning and introducing harmony into the Church. The organist being away on a holiday, and having to sing without musical accompaniment, we thought it a good opportunity to try, at least, one hymn in four parts; the "Old Hundredth" was selected for the first, and to be sung when the Vicar went into the vestry to change his surplice for his gown, in which to preach the sermon, as was the custom in those days. I was to blow the key note with a "pitch pipe"; this I did, and all took up, and sustained their parts well. The congregation turned round and faced us, en masse. The Vicar came out of the vestry looking with astonishment, and as black (metaphorically) as the gown he had just put on, and immediately dispatched his clerk with a message for our leader, Henry Overington, to attend in the vestry at the close of the service. Seeing that the Vicar was displeased with the innovation, the hymn at the end of the service was of course sung in the usual way. Our leader, as desired, went into the vestry and the rest of the choir awaited the verdict. On his return, he stated that the Vicar asked him*

*what we were singing, our leader said "I told him we were singing the old hundredth in four parts, and I thought it went very well"; the Vicar replied, "I don't profess to know much about music, it might have gone very well, but don't do it again." Little clusters gathered together, on their way home after the service that day, discussing the merits or demerits of the singing. One old man was heard to say to another, "What was the matter with the singers today then?" the other replied, "I dun know, some was singen one toon and some was singen another, and Edward Sayers was gwain to play some sort of insterment, but he broke down fust noat." So we continued in unison with our singing, as well as with our Vicar, a few years longer.*

The pitch pipe that Edward used can still be seen in the case outside the vestry of the church, together with some of the instruments that were used by the church band in the nineteenth century. Part singing was, of course, ultimately accepted, and today, as well as a thriving traditional choir, the church is the home of Jubilate, a choir that gives a program of concerts locally, in aid of various charities.

Edward Sayers was also a bellringer, and in this he was following a tradition which dates back to the sixteenth century. The churchwardens' accounts make continual reference from 1518 onwards [126] to expenditure connected with the bells of Tarring church, including the making of new bell ropes and a new clapper for the great bell, and in 1531, one of the bells was taken down and removed to the bellfounders. This was not a long journey, since Topsell's bell foundry was at that time situated behind what is now known as Church Cottage, on the north side of Church Road. The foundry flourished until at least the beginning of the seventeenth century, and bells made here can still be found in Bury and Felpham, and even as far afield as Hastings.

There were five bells and a sanctus bell in 1533, but in the nineteenth century, two were damaged by young boys, pupils of the vicar. They tied whipcord around them and then rang the bells, causing them to crack. The remaining three bells were chimed by three boys, of whom Edward Sayers was one, in 1853. In 1926, as an old man with a shaky hand, he remembered that they were chimed with ropes tied to their clappers, and wrote [127]:

*I Edward Sayers the first bell did ring*
*With a high pitched note which seemed to say DING*
*The second by Frederick Willis Long*
*Had a deeper tone and seemed to say DONG*
*While Thomas Tap Chipper with the big bell*
*Completed the full rounds of DING,DONG,DELL.*

The old bells were taken down near the end of 1853, and recast into the six smaller ones which hang in the tower today. This time, however, the work had to be done by Messrs Mears of London, since Topsell's foundry had disappeared over two hundred years earlier. The new bells were hung in the traditional way, attached to large wheels, and with their mouths pointing upwards, so that they could be swung full circle with ropes, whereas the previous bells had apparently hung downwards, and could only be tolled by means of a rope attached to the clapper. Edward was soon back in the belfrey, learning to ring them properly. He admits, however, that he was too

*71. The church seen from the south before the alterations, which included the addition of the vestry, in 1853.*

*72. A drawing of the church from the north in 1851.*

short to reach the end of the rope at the back stroke, and had to stand on a stool. He continued as a ringer for over a quarter of a century. The bells were once again tuned and rehung [128] in 1955.

The recasting of the bells in 1853 was part of a major restoration of the church [129] undertaken at a cost of £2200, much of which was raised by the vicar, Revd J. W. Warter. A new vestry on the south side was built, and the interior extensively altered to remove piecemeal alterations of previous years, and return the building to a homogeneous whole. After seven months work, the restored church was reopened on Palm Sunday, 1854. Later in the year, the work was completed with the installation of a new organ, to replace the earlier eighteenth century instrument [130].

The new bells brought a poignant pleasure to an old lady in the following year, 1855, when William Whitehead of Salvington married a Miss Browning of London in Tarring church [131]. The bridegroom's mother was very ill, and had been lingering in a hopeless condition for some weeks. Nevertheless, since she was in favour of the

*73. The Apostle mosaics in the nave of the church. The lower photograph shows the fourteenth century chest in which the parish records were kept.*

marriage, she insisted that the ceremony took place immediately. She directed that the windows of her chamber be opened, and the last thing she was heard to say was - "the bells" - as the marriage peal for her son floated into the death chamber of his mother. She died shortly after receiving this evidence of the accomplishment of her last wish.

The exterior of the church has changed little since this restoration, other than the addition of the lychgate in the present century. Inside, the chancel roof was strengthened in 1952, and a new reredos added. The oak screen at the west end was installed in 1965. The organ, which had been renewed in 1863, was replaced with a modern instrument in 1958. The weathercock, which was made by Hollands the smith in 1809, was repaired in 1884 by his descendant John Hollands, having been damaged through target practice by the guns of local residents!

The oldest part of the church is the nave, which dates from the end of the thirteenth century, although the roof was substantially repaired in the nineteenth century. The chancel and the tower were added in the early years of the fifteenth century, and the screen is also of about this date. The six clergy stalls have misericords, which are hinged wooden seats. When raised, the undersides reveal narrow ledges which, with care, can be sat on, while continuing to give the impression of standing. These must have been invaluable during long sermons, but there was a catch. The seats are delicately balanced, and if the occupant were to nod off to sleep, the seat was liable to fall down with an enormous clatter! The carpenter who carved the seat was traditionally allowed free reign in the choice of subject for the underside of the ledge. In many misericords this resulted in grotesque and often irreligious representations, but the carvers in Tarring seem to have been a pious lot: the carvings are limited to foliage and two old mens' heads.

*74. The church roof collapsed, possibly late in the last century, as this photograph shows.*

The structure has been described as a "twelve apostle church". With five arches on each side, and one at each of the tower and chancel ends, there are twelve arches in total, and there are indeed nineteenth century Italian mosaics of the twelve apostles around the nave. All of the stained glass in the church is relatively modern. The windows commemorating St Richard of Chichester and St Thomas of Canterbury were dedicated in 1958. The Henty window at the side of the altar, and the west window commemorating the poet Southey, father-in-law of the then vicar, J. W. Warter, are from the nineteenth century. The Victorian font replaced an older one, which went to Australia with the Hentys, and stood for many years in Melbourne cathedral.

A full list of the incumbents of the vicarage and rectory of Tarring, and of the ancient chantry of St Mary, is included in Appendix 2.

CHAPTER ELEVEN

# THE BLACK LION

Although the farmhouse of Church Farm was on the south side of Church Road, the farm yard and buildings were on the north, under what is now Church Way. They extended as far as Bellview Road, which was, until this century, a narrow lane leading to Salvington. The farm itself was extensive, running to 280 acres. It reached to the parish boundary in the west, the Littlehampton Road in the north, the line of the railway in the south, and included two thirds of the land in the parish between the railway and the sea.

In around 1850, the vicar took a walk from Tarring with a friend, and his descriptions [132] show just how much things have changed in the last 150 years:

*From Tarring to Durrington is a long mile and a half; and the direct path is across that magnificent field adjoining the church - than which there may be as fine, but there is no finer, land in England. It is not uncommonly known as Markwick's big field.*

From here, they walked to Patching, down through Castle Goring woods to the sea, and along the coast to Heene. The description continues:

*Instead of going direct to the Heene Lane which runs right through the village, and has now, from carelessness, become a road, whereas formerly it was for the use of the farm only and the inhabitants, we turned across the lands which bear the name of the Heene Common, intersected with sea ditches, and well bestrewed with gorse. Before us lay the chapel and the farm, and on our right the hamlet...Instead of following the road to Tarring, we diverged from the chapel-yard to the great Heene field, and from thence we gazed on the dear old church with delight, seldom seen with more effect than when the purple light of eve rests upon its time-worn tower, and shingled spire that points to heaven. At any time the church of West Tarring is seen to great advantage from the small path that leads towards it from the mill.*

*75. This old thatched barn, built of wood on stone foundations, stood in the farmyard of Church Farm, on the site of what is now Church Way. The lower photograph is an interior view.*

We can see that, at the time, Tarring was a compact village, surrounded on all sides by fields, and it remained so until the present century. The villages of Heene, Durrington and Salvington were similar, but much smaller. To the east of Tarring, the fields were the original open fields of the manor, and apart from Heene mill, there were no buildings between the village, Heene and Broadwater. The fields to the west of the church were demsne lands, and there were very few buildings in them 150 years ago.

Chippers Castle, an attractive flint cottage which still stands in Castle Road, was built probably around the beginning of the nineteenth century as a farmworker's cottage. It was occupied in 1841 by Thomas Chipper, his wife Mary and their five children. It doesn't seem to have had any further connection with the Chipper family, but it is still called Chippers Cottage, and the names Chipper and Castle dominate the street names around. At the turn of the century there was a pond nearby on the south side, but it seems to have dried up subsequently, and was eventually built over. Castle Road was also the home of Worthing Rugby Club before its move to new grounds in Roundstone Lane, Angmering in 1979.

Lincett Barn, which stood on the site of the houses on the north side of Princess Avenue, also had ponds close by. Most villages had brickworks in the nineteenth century - there were 180 in Sussex alone - and Tarring was no exception. The Tarring Brickworks stood here, north of the railway, and the bricks were laid out in the brickfields north of Canterbury Road to dry, prior to firing. The works had moved from its earlier site closer to the railway to make way for the goods yard.

Since the vicar's walk, the extensive demesne lands of Church Farm have been progressively developed, although even in 1956, the Worthing Directory states the chief crops of the parish to be *wheat, barley, oats, turnips, mangold wurzel and peas.* Today, however, there is no farmland at all in Tarring.

The growth of what is now West Worthing began with the appointment of the West Worthing Improvement Commissioners in 1865. This body took over the local government of the area, and began a carefully planned development. They had grandiose plans, as the following extract [133] from a local paper of 1884 shows:

*76. This drawing, by A. Elliot in 1920, show how Tarring was still a country village then. It shows the view of the church from across Markwick's big field, from what is now the top of Lindum Road. The lower photograph shows how different the view is today.*

*A few weeks since, it was rumoured in the town that the valuable and extensive Freehold Building Estate at Heene (containing about one hundred and seventy acres) had been purchased by a London merchant - we are now able to confirm this large transaction, and as the matter is one intimately associated with the development and prosperity of the town, we give a few particulars of this fine property. The Estate is situate on the west side of Heene Road, and is bounded on the north by the main line of the London, Brighton, and South Coast Railway; it has a southern aspect, and extends to the West Worthing Esplanade. The views inland are unsurpassed for beauty on the entire south coast and the extensive sea view in uninterrupted as far as to the Isle of Wight. The handsome new Church and Rectory at Heene stand nearly in the centre of the Estate. A number of new wide roads have recently been completed on the east side of the property, and first-class villas built, which are nearly all let. There is an excellent supply of water, gas lamps and postal pillar boxes in all the new roads, and the drainage is perfect. A few large plots,from an acre to three acres each, were sold last summer to several London gentlemen, the price paid varying from £700 to £1000 per acre, according to position, the vendors stipulating that first-class villas shall be built. We believe it is the intention of the purchaser to fully develop the property, and to at once open the road known as the Grand Avenue, running through the Estate, from the railway near Tarring crossing to the Esplanade; this road, which is eighty feet wide, will, when completed and connected with the Parade, give to Worthing one of the finest drives in the kingdom.*

Subsequently, of course, many of these villas have been replaced by larger blocks of flats, and the views to all sides have been obscured by further development. Nevertheless, Grand Avenue remains a "grand" drive, as was originally intended. The fields to the west of South Street have been gradually taken over by more intensive housing in the present century.

The houses on the west side of St Andrews Road were the scene of the largest bombing raid on Worthing in the second war, when on December 3rd 1940, 19 incendiary bombs fell in their back gardens. Fortunately, many of them failed to explode, and little damage resulted, either to people or to property. This was not the case almost

*77. A watercolour showing Tarring Church in the distance across the fields. It was painted from south west of the church, near Lincett barn. The pond was one of many produced by the waters of the Teville stream, which originally flowed across these fields, but is now controlled in an underground pipe.*

a year later, however, when two much larger high explosive bombs fell on houses in Haynes Road on the night of November 1st 1941. Seven lives were lost, and twenty nine people required hospital treatment. This was the worst incident experienced in the Worthing area during the whole of the war.

Tarring suffered during the war because it was on one of the direct routes of bombers from the continent, but this was by no means the first time that its location had led to problems of enemy attack. We have seen that the vulnerability of the coastline gave rise to the Tarring market petition of 1444, and it continued to be a problem throughout the next century.

Concerned over the threat of an invasion by Spain, Elizabeth I commissioned a survey of the coast in 1587. A well-drawn, but rather rudimentary map is accompanied by a description of the coast and the landing conditions [134]. Describing the coast between Littlehampton and Shoreham, it says:

*betwene littel Hampton and Shoreham gode landing for the most parte, viz. at Kingston Stade, and so to Goringe Beacons, and therefore to be flancked and Trenched. And in like sorte notwithstandinge that there is good landinge betwene these Beacons and Shoreham, yet the Cooste is reasonably well gardid, viz. betwene Goringe and Heinde mille with a water betwene the Beache and the firme lande save only next the mille and that muddy and growen with sedges. Also betwene this and Worthinge beacons is an old small trenche in Cheverne (chevron) forme, wch may be strengthened by retrenchinge and flankinge of the same artificially.*

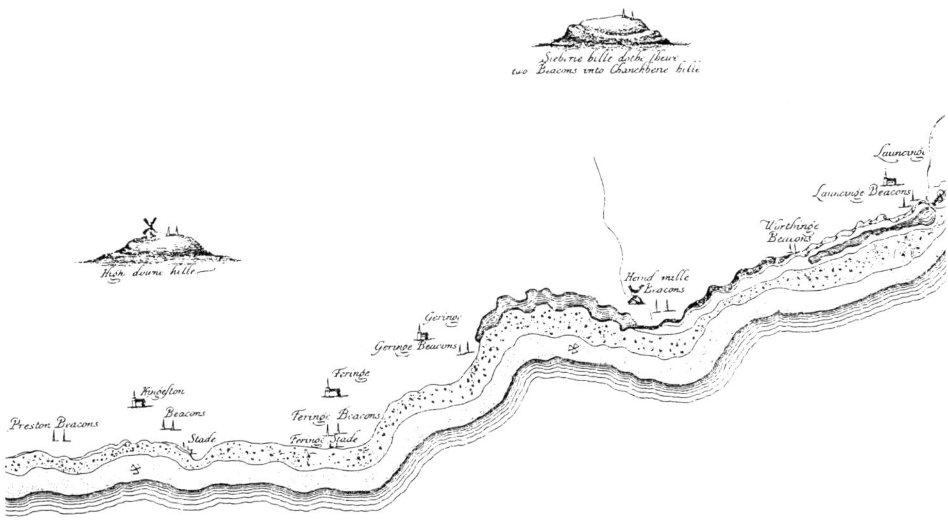


*78. The coast as surveyed in 1587 for Queen Elizabeth I, in preparation for the arrival of the Spanish Armada.*

This map does not seem to confirm the often repeated story that Tarring church tower was used as a lookout for the Armada [135]. There was also a story current earlier this century, although since discredited, that because of its service as an armada lookout, Tarring church was entitled to fly the White Ensign, the flag of the Royal Navy, from its tower [136].

The connection of Tarring with the sea goes back far earlier than the Armada, however. In 1842, during a storm, an ancient boat was revealed in the mud of the shore off the end of Heene Road, [137]. It had been carved, or dug out, from the trunk of a single oak tree, either by burning or by using primitive tools, and did not contain any metal in its construction. Unfortunately, the boat itself is now lost, but from this description, and contemporary examination, we can presume it was of pre-Roman origin. A boat of similar age was found [138] in North Stoke on the Arun in 1834, and is preserved in the British Museum. It measured 10.6 metres in length, and between 0.8 and 1.4 metres in width. Its maximum depth was 0.8 metres, and it contained three partitions, which served to strengthen the sides and provide seats for the crew.

*79. This boat, made from the trunk of a single oak tree, was uncovered by a storm on the beach south of Heene Road in 1842. It dates from before the Roman conquest.*

The line of the coast here, and hence the extent of the parish and manor, has been changing constantly over the centuries. As early as 1341, a tax return [139] pleaded the poverty of the village through failure of the crops due to bad weather and *certain lands sown, which were destroyed by the irruption of the sea, to the loss of 6s 8d.* Later, in 1724, a map [140] contained an inscription - *It appears by an inscription at Heene Parsonage, that since the year 1699, the Sea has gain'd on that Coast 6 Perches* (about 30 metres).

In the mid-nineteenth century, the sea road to Worthing was twice swallowed up by the sea, and 11 metres of ground were lost [141].

Earlier, land had existed at what was then low-water mark, and James Carter, who died in about 1849, remembered sowing wheat and ploughing in the seafields of Tarring where there was now only sand [142]. In 1817, it was said that many old people remembered houses standing in Worthing *at the spot which is now low water-mark* [143]. Earlier, in 1755, a tenant had stood at high-water mark and remembered playing cricket there [144]. At the time, the sea was so far away that no one ever struck a ball into it! Adding these fragments of information together, we can see that a substantial amount of land was lost in the seventeenth and eighteenth centuries. The incursion was only halted with the construction of the groynes in the mid-nineteenth century.

*80. These three cottages in Church Road replaced the old Black Lion inn in 1839.*

Returning to our walk, as we move back towards the market-place from the site of Church Farm, we find three flint-faced cottages. The one on the left is known as Church Cottage and that on the right, Artists Cottage, possibly after the artist E.L.J.Harris, who lived here in 1960. Previously, all three were known as Church Cottages, and before that Church Street Cottages.

The cottages as they now appear were constructed in around 1839, probably using the frame of an earlier timber-framed building, which was, in 1658, a house with *a garden and backside at the farm gate in Tarring*. It was owned by William Fletcher, who also owned the George, then called the White Horse, and occupied by Thomas Farnecombe. By 1674, the house had become an inn called the Black Lion, and remained so until 1770, when it became the Black Horse. This was about the same time that the White Horse became the George. The change of name suggests that it was still in operation as an inn at this time. The house continued to be described as the Black Horse until 1839, when it was rebuilt as three separate private houses.

Behind the Black Lion was a small plot of ground measuring 14 by 9 metres on which stood a small cottage, which in the sixteenth century had been the home of Thomas Topsell, the bell founder. During the last century, it was occupied by James Long, who was parish clerk for many years before his death in 1847. His work was much appreciated by the vicar, John Warter, who wrote of him [145]:

> *Seventy and five years, man and boy, he has heard these Church bells call to prayer; forty and five years he has officiated as clerk and sexton. When his turn to depart comes, I question if his place will be better filled. Obstinate, at times, as a quadruped I need not name, he is shrewd and intelligent, plain-spoken and trustworthy.*

He was buried in the churchyard, where his grave bore the inscription [146]:

> *James Long born October 13 1770, died March 10 1847.*
> *fifty years Clerk of this Parish.*
> *God be merciful to me a sinner.*

The cottage had disappeared by 1875, and the land was then used as an orchard attached to the house to the west of the Black Lion. It seems that this was also the site of the Tarring bell foundry.

The street frontage from here to the George has all been redeveloped in the last hundred years, and apart from the remains of some old flint walls in the rear gardens, little trace of the older buildings remains.

*81. Mascot Works, the home of the Whitehouse sweet factory, just before its sale, and conversion to a private house, in the 1960's.*

The first two houses, originally called Southview and Cranbourne Villa, date from the turn of the century. After the war, Cranbourne Villa was the home of Mascot Works, where J. Whitehouse and Co. manufactured sweets. The sweet factory closed in the sixties [147], and in 1980 a terrace of houses was built on the rear of the site, with access from Church Way. The house itself had by this time returned to use as a private home.

The terrace of houses numbers 81 to 91 was also built in the early years of this century. Originally, they all had names; starting from the west, Belmont, Ivydean, Jessamine, Albury, Denmead and Briars. Jesamine was divided into two cottages for a time in the twenties and thirties, and Ivydean was briefly a motor coach garage in around 1936. Briars was occupied from its construction by William Batten and later by his son Robert William Batten, who still lived here in 1960.

Before this terrace was built, this was the site of a seventeenth century shopping centre known as the Shambles, an old English word meaning a butcher's slaughter house or a meat market. There were three shops, two houses and a malthouse here in 1650 and six shops in 1839. The tithe map suggests that they were set back from the road in a sort of early shopping precinct. Soon afterwards, the shops were closed and converted to private houses, and remained so until they were demolished ninety years ago. We know little about these shops, except that one was a shoemaker's in 1839.

# CONCLUSION

And now we have arrived back at the George and Dragon, the point where we began. Standing on the corner here, we can see a considerable portion of the modern village, and from what we have discovered, we can imagine what we would have seen if we had stood here at other times in the past.

Looking up the High Street in 1839, we notice surprisingly little difference. There are no street lights or road signs of course, and the road is not paved. It is very muddy, and liberally scattered with horse manure. Right at the top of the street, we can just see Edward Hollands' blacksmith's shop.

*82. An early photograph of the upper end of the High Street. Stents Cottages are in the foreground, and all of the houses in view are thatched.*

Directly in front of us, Parsonage Row continues south to the farm gate which leads to the Old Palace grounds. There is a butcher's shop here with meat hanging in its open windows, and the smell of baking bread comes from the bakery. On the other side of the gate, the sounds of the washerwoman at work come from the rather decayed building known as the episcopal brewhouse.

Through the gate, the Old Palace stands surrounded by garden, and we can see the two huge tithe barns which are now a little dilapidated, since they are no longer needed to store the church share of the produce of the village.

Looking down South Street, past the gate to the vicarage on the left and the stone-healed house on the right, we can see the newly built house called Pendules and the old thatched roof of Haynes Cottage.

*83. The market-place in about 1890, before the south gable of Parsonage Row fell into disrepair.*

On our right, the shops in the Market House are open, and turning further to look down the narrow Church Lane, we can see The Old Cottage, and past it the gate to the manor house. There is much activity in the yard of Church Farm, and right behind us, people come and go to the shops in the Shambles.

The men are wearing coloured cloth coats, with boots and knee breeches, the ladies narrow dresses with high waists and puffed sleeves, with large bonnets, or caps tied under the chin. All in all, a busy small town, one of the most important in the district.

Now let us imagine it is about 1650. Parsonage Row looks much the same, except that the shops have drop-down shutters rather than windows. High Street still has houses along both sides as far as we can see, but they are all timber-framed buildings, not black and white but lime washed all over. They have mostly thatched roofs, with the occasional one of Horsham stone. There are fewer houses, and more gaps between then to give access to the fields behind. Looking down South Street, we see only the occasional thatched house, with extensive open fields around.

*84. A steam lorry making a delivery to the George and Dragon in the early years of this century. The sign on the wall on the left points "to the church and footpaths only".*

On our right, the new Market House built by Thomas Botting is open and, since it is Saturday, the corn market is in full swing, with men and boys from all over the county, on horses and in carts, coming and going. The two inns, the Ship in Church Lane and the White Horse beside us are doing a roaring trade, and William Fletcher is thinking about opening a third, the Black Lion, at his house near the farm gate. The visitors are also providing good trade for the shops behind us in the Shambles, and everywhere groups of people stand exchanging news. There are about 150 families living in Tarring, in about 70 houses.

Going back to the Middle Ages, in about 1300, we can only speculate as to what we might see from our vantage point. The Old Palace, looking much as it does six hundred years later, is the centre of the village. As well as the building itself, there are a number of other cottages surrounding it, and with its high wall, the settlement is well protected from potential foreign raiders. There are some other houses outside the wall, but in these times, buildings are generally not designed to have long lives.

On our left, a few houses flank the rough and muddy track that leads to the north. It is along here that the archbishop will come, with his retinue, on one of his regular visits, being transported by the men of the village which he has last visited. It will be an opportunity to exchange news, and the men know that when the time comes for the

*85. One of the first motor buses to take over the popular horse-drawn bus service between Tarring and Worthing, shown here picking up passengers in front of the Parish Reading Room in the market-place.*

archbishop to leave, it will be their turn to help transport the household to the next residence, perhaps at Pagham or South Malling.

Behind the Palace we can see men working their land in the Town Field, one of the three large fields surrounding the village. Along the lane leading to the church are some more houses, and the church itself.

The further we go back in time, the less evidence we have, and the harder it becomes to imagine what the village would have looked like. Going back to the year 1000, we have no local evidence at all, and we must rely on more general historical data. Almost certainly there was a church here then, and the excavations on the site of Church House show evidence of twelfth century occupation close by. Probably the paths to Salvington and Durrington in the nineteenth century existed then too, together with the one to Goring, an extension of Church Lane which was later cut off by the enclosure of the demesne farm land. The fact that these paths, and the eastern ones to Heene and Broadwater converge on the church suggests that this was probably the centre of the Saxon village. In fact, the corner we are standing on may not even have been a street corner at all at this time.

*86. South Street, looking south from the market-place. The house on the right is the stone-healed house.*

However, close to the church, we can certainly see about twenty small huts. For the most part they are ramshackle affairs, consisting of one small room where the whole family lives, eats and sleeps. The smoke from the central fires which burn in the middle of the floors of the huts can be seen rising from holes in the thatched roofs, and the walls are made of crudely interlaced sticks, covered with dried mud. Each hut is between ten and twenty feet in length and breadth, and provides accomodation not only for the family but also for its animals.

In the fields around, there are no hedges, but the land is divided into strips separated by low banks of soil. The village must survive on the food it can grow in these fields, so co-operation is essential. There is very little contact with the outside world, and strangers are treated with suspicion, since the village has suffered from sporadic Viking raids for as long as anyone can remember. The village as it looks now is not so very different from the first settlement built here by the descendants of Teorra five hundred years before.

*87. Church Lane, Tarring, early in the present century. There is no footpath on the north of the street.*

And so we return to the present day. Over the fifteen hundred years that people have lived here, the village has been constantly changing. It is sad that sometimes such changes have resulted in the loss of buildings that could have been preserved, but we are fortunate to have retained more than most. Change will continue, since it is both necessary and inevitable; who would want now to live in one of those mud and straw huts that Teorra built so long ago? But with our current interest in conservation, we can be sure that the best of our ancient heritage will be preserved, so that our children and grandchildren can relate to the past through more than just the written word.

I hope you have enjoyed our walk together through the history of Tarring, and that as you make your way through the village in future, you will see it with a new eye. I trust, too, that you will spare a thought for the many people who have lived here before us, and created the history of our village, just as we are continuing to do today.

APPENDIX ONE

# TARRING PEOPLE

**Tenants owing service according to the custumal [148] of 1282**

William Wildegos
William Le Wolf
Edward Carpentarius
John de Sunting
John Jaoer
William Wylteschir'
Agnes widow of Bugon'
William Cusyn'
Joan Aber
John le Fry
Richard son of Stephen le Mascon'
Richard Carpentarius
John Kente
Alice de Suthetone
William Bykeley
Roger Belle
Maud at Watersipe
Adam at Estetone
Clemence daughter of Wylekyn'
Ralph Kent
Stephen Echman'
Andrew Bollyng
Richard Weylomer
Nicholas Abbot
Geoffrey Jolip
Adam le Il
Thomas at See
Widow Burri
Walter Cacher
widow of the shepherd
Thomas Spyght
John de Mari
Robert Zenell
Christine de Wetersipe
Juliana Consutrix
Roger Randolf
Ralph Mercator
Walter Wisman
Thomas le Walys
Thomas Carpenter
Stephen at Feld
Adam Busch'
Adam a Northe'ton'
Walter Michel
Agnes widow of Lucas
Norman Bykeley
Richard Colstable
Simon at Pette
Richard Longus
Robert Adam
John Faber
Simon Thedolf'
Margery in Thehale
Richard Sweyne
Roger Thedoulf
William Palmere
Thomas Fall
widow of Thomas Godwyne
widow of Godfrey Gule
Widow Buchard
Agatha Malger
Walter Hurlebat

**Owners of property subject to the subsidy tax [149] of 1296**

Ricard' le Porter
Ricard' Hayne
Domino Johanne capellanus *(vicar)*
Johanne Taylur
Martin' Hayne

**Owners of property subject to the subsidy tax [150] of 1327**

Thom' Coteman
Walto Kente
Rogo Soutere
Alic' a Northetone
Robto Method
Johne Kente
Joh' Brac'
Thom' a Nestetoune
Willo Adam
Rico le Longe
Rico in the Hale
Walto a Southetoun
Johe atte Lithe
Rico Crol
Relicta Bacheler
Godefro Brut
Relicta Bykeley
Relicta Wybelyn
Agn' Janyng
Relicta Gol
Godefro Wybelyn

**Parishioners subject to the lay subsidy [151] of 1524**

John Gylmyn
John Stacey
Jefferay Turnageyn
Thomas Shorte
*His servants*
  John Bradbryge
  John Blakor
  Wyllyam Rawkyn
  John Potte, a ducheman
  Deryk Thyn, a ducheman
Thomas Kyngeston
Rychard Blake
Thomas Lynster
John Jenyn hys seruant
George Hunt
Nycholas Carew
John Copden
Mylys Meryfeld
John Fogyn, a Norman
Edward Weston
John Hall
Rychard Marche
Thomas Wulrygge hys servant
John Perys
Thomas Marche
Rychard Parker
Robert Perys
John Kyngeston
Wyllyam Turneageyn
Thomas Wolder
Thomas Harmede
Thomas Stacy
John Balsheff
John Pulman
John Fayrewether
Thomas Hunt
Wyllyam Blakman
Rychard Bull
John Bron
Thomas Kellowe
Rychard Hamper
Wyllyam Tylar
Wyllyam Strengar
Thomas Trollopp
Edward Terell
Adam Apkyn
Robert Marten
Rychard Raynold
Rychard Grevett
John Bounde
John Wulfyn
Robert Pycas
Thomas Penyale
John Furne
Rychard Fayrewether
Nycholas a Felde
John Turnageyn
John Stere
John Wase
Gyles Nores, a gasken
Wyllyam Palyngham
Thomas Garry
John a Felde
Wyllyam Molde
Thomas Hamper
...trett Fyssicyon

**Parishioners subject to the landscote tax [152] of 1581**

Edmane Derring
Thom's hatch
Richard Mase
Thomas Selden
John Edenes
Richard Cookes
Will' Selden
Mychelle Hyd
Richard Nashe
Richard Lucas
Richard Stammer
John Gosman
Charles biship
Henry Gattes
John Darknalle
John Waller
John pearse
Barnard Warwicke
Ed Kingsto'
John ffallck
Chayger
Henry Walder
Thomas Gattes
Thomas Selden
Roger Kingston
Will Clarke
John fflecher
Richard Huden
Henry Cookes
Will' Parsson
John Hamper
Thomas Hamper
Selden
Warrell
Richard Huden
John Symsson
Thomas Wesson
John Selden
Henry Steter
John Hunte
John Hardman
Moyshese Derring
Richard Cooke
Edward Wase
Will Parker
James Grave
Smyth Wido
John Graves
Thomas Kember
Thomas Tayler
Gerred Yonge
John Wiseman
Roger Waterffyld
Robert Smyth
Henrye barnard
Thomas Umfery
John Stone
Thomas Lucas
John Smyth
Turnagayns Wido
Will Samson
John Wicken
John fflecher ye elder
Richard Shorte
Thomas Kynte
Henry Porchester
Raph Wynkfelde
Wedo Clark
John hobyohn
Henry Gravat
John Selden
Thomas Boncar
philyp Lucas
Richard Cooke
Robert bailar
Thomas ffylde
John Donsould
Edmond Passon
John Hobyohn
Richard Marsh
Henry Steters mother
Richard Hamper
Belchamber

**Survey [153] of tenants of the manor in c1610**

Henry Heather
John Willett
Henry Mitchell
Brian Voices
Thos Avenett
John Foices
Edrus Pilfold
Thos Patching
Edrus Pilfold
Ricus Horley
Edrus Wicker
Lodovicus Hendries
Margaret Selden
Walterr Gibbon
Bernard Warwick
Richard Futter
Alicia Humphrey
Beatrix Smith
Nicholas Bell
John Munnery
Ellienora Evans
Robert Owdler
John Wheatley
Johanne Reade
John Hornsby
Jacob Grave
Thomas Fletcher
Jacob Chates
Joanna Hamper
Henry Cook
Edrus Parsons
Benjamin Olliver
Jacob Graves
Henry Dorchester
Avisia Harman
Thos Barnard
Samuel Selden
John Marsh
Humphrey Booth
John Ravenscroft
Jacob Allen
Henry Napper
Thos Sawyer
Joanna Mounck
Thos Herst
Nicholas Comber
Nicholas Mitchell
Richard Gratwick
Maria Edsall
Egidus Vates
Rudulph Wingfield
John Fallick
John Lucas
Thos Wilkins
John Rose
John Hide
Richard Streeter
Richard Peeter
Henry Paynot
John Selden
Thos Gratwick
Moses Brian
Edrus Weston
Roger Carpenter
Robert Houlden
William Selden
Thos Weston
John Warrell
Jacob Gravel
Geo Hamper
John Parson
Thos Warden
Johanna Lech
Ricus Streeter
Thos Selden
Robert Floates
Richard Topsell

**Parishioners in the protestation return [154] of 1641**

Wm Stanley,Minister*
Thomas South*
Willi; Fletcher*
Wm Warrell
Robert Porchester
Thomas Warrell
George Goringe*
Willi; Hide*
Edward Cooke*
John Tayler
John Cristopher
Robert Holnye
Richard Grinfeld*
John Frances
John Hornbe*
Rich; Dudman
Richard Nashe
Thomas Nashe
William Nash*
James Sumner*
Jousef Lester*
John Blake
Thomas Marks
John Cooper
Benjamin Smith*
William Seeman
James South*
Moyses Cristopher
Richerd Wease
Bartholme Modey
Richerd Wease
John Harman
Willia; Cooke*
Richard Knight*
Richerd Harowde
Willi: Durante
Edward Cooke*
Thomas Cooke*
John Tufe
Richerd Fisher
Richerd Slater
John Swifte
John Longemor
Robert Manerey
Thomas Spring, sen
Nicho: Godward
Nicho: Trate
John Bash*
Thomas Faromcome*
Thomas Beard
Moyses Dudman
Charles Johnson*
Thomas Botting*
Thomas Bellchamber
John Harwood*
Peeter Chiper*
Thomas Paysie
William Wheatley*
Richerd Stumer
Antonie Walter
John White*
John Ampellford
Nicho; Carden
Thomas Barnard
Allen Larkin
John Inesley
Thomas Olliver*
John Peter*
Thomas Tailor*
John Tailor*
Thomas Sherlock
John Faulkner
John Heathe
Richerd Cearden
Clement Quinbey
John Stapler
John Hamper*
Thomas Swifte
Thomas Legett,sen
Thomas Legett,jur
John Stoneham
Thomas Easton
John Stapler
Richerd Carver
Robert Weston*
John Pollard*
John Edwardes
Edman Edwardes
Nicholas Farlye
John Manser
Edward Munnare*
Thomas Capelin
Mathew Peeter
Richerd Hilles
Antonie Voakes
Thomas Voakes
Robert Emery
Rafe Tilley
Richerd Emerey
William Hamper
Richard Weeston*
Thomas Stone
William Fivenes sen.
William Fivens jur*
John Hoseyer
Edward Terell
George chiper
John Ouden
Richerd Farlye
John Oulsonn
Humphree Selden
John Duey
John Dudman
John Stapler
Edward Graves
James Graves*
Richerd Preste
Roger Hodges
John Houlden
Richerd Warell
Michael Wheatley*
Thomas Blackman
Richerd Horowde
William Avere
Samuell Wodger
Thomas Jones
Thomas Goulde
James Burden
John Souten
Richerd Ayleing
Siperen Tearle
Philipp Capon
Benjamine Eliott*
Richard Knighte, sen*
Richard Hamper*
Richard Paine
John Pollard
William Morman
William Rigate
Robert Joanes

Richerd Cooke
Lement Hilan*
Roberte French
William, Tillsey
Phillip Stumer
Edward Swifte
Thomas Ayleward
Edward Democke
Henerey Hobejohn
William Bacon
John Hilles
Edward Dimmucke
Reynold Warrell
Thomas Eliott
Thomas Warrell
Thomas Poter

*(* indicates those who signed their own names - 41 out of 156)*

**Property owners subject to the hearth tax [155] of 1662**

Thomas Dale cler
George Fletcher gen
Henry Stiles
Mich Pi..
Thomas Shearlock
John Jupe
William Patching
Robert Firens
Mary Peter
Thomas Johnsen
William Taylor
Matthew Nye
John Champion
James Graves
Margery Harwood
Robert Dudman
Elizabeth Botting wid
William Hamper
JohnFish
John Cooper
Richard Grinsted
William Worrell
John Parson
Richard Waterfield
John Heares
Thomas Hamper
John Moulson jr
John Selden
Edward Tanner
George Phippes
Robert Firens
William Edwards
6 names erased
William Wheatley gen
George Fletcher jun
James South
Thomas ffarncombe
Henry Phillips
Allen Larkins
George Puttocke
Joane Wheatly
George Hide
Edward Gates
Richard Nash
Richard Beard
James Challoner
Thomas Taylor
Thomas Whittington
John Hide
John Heath
Peter Chipper
James Graves
Robert Yalden
Thomas Markes
Edward Weston
Elizabeth Breist
Sarah Thorne
Thomas Boakes
John Moulson
Mary Blake
Daniell Wase
Richard Weston
John Noakes
William Avere
John Clere

**Owners and occupiers of property in the land tax return [156] of 1780**

| *Proprietor* | *Occupier* |
|---|---|
| Thos Brigs for his house | James Andrews |
| Ann Vowler for her farm | John Barker |
| James Margesson for his farm | John Barker |
| John Barker for his land | himself |
| John Meredew for his house | Soloman Burchall |
| Ann & Martha Butler for a croft | Wm Bartley |
| Josiah Munery for a croft | Geo Bushby |
| William Challen for his house | himself |
| Richard Chapman for his house | himself |
| Thomas Clear for his land | Martha Pelling |
| William Puttick for his house | Richard Emory |
| Richard Edmunds for his house | himself |
| Richard Edmunds for his house | Thomas Thorpe |
| John Crofts for his land | George Feast |
| William Grevatt for his house&land | himself |
| Mariah Hedgcock for her house | herself |
| Mariah Hedgcock for another house | Thos Richardson |
| William Bartley for his house | Edwd Andrews |
| Thomas Heward for his house | himself |
| Allen Hide for his house | himself |
| John Harris for his house | himself |
| William Penfold for his house | James Jones |
| William Cooper for his house | Humph'y Latter |
| Henry Lindup for his land | himself |
| John Long for his house | himself |
| John Long junr for his house | himself |
| William Lelliot for his house | himself |
| John Markwick for his house | himself |
| Joseph Moore for his salary | |
| William Newman for his land | himself |
| Edward Barker for his farm | William Penfold |
| Revd Jeremiah Mills for the Parsonage | William Penfold |
| Edmund Parker for his house | himself |
| Martha Pelling for her farm | herself |
| Abigail Puttock for her house | John Lindup |
| Richard Pannet for his house | himself |
| Thomas Pullen for his house | himself |
| Richard Michell for his house | himself |
| Revd Dr Rycroft for his Vicarage | Peter Penfold |
| Willm Richardson for part of Field Place | Geo Oliver |
| Barnard Rye for her house | herself |
| James Russell for his house | John Russell |
| James Carter for his house | himself |
| Ann Herriot for her house | Joseph Moore |
| Ann Cousins for her house | herself |

| | |
|---|---|
| John Sayres for his house | himself |
| Henry Pelling for his house & land | himself |
| John Sayres junr for his farm | himself |
| Thomas Haines for his farm | Willm Shepherd |
| Ann Ford for her land | Will Shepherd |
| James Street for his house | himself |
| John Meredew for his house | John Street |
| Thomas Short for his house | himself |
| Willm Tribe for his house & land | himself |
| Thomas Tate for his house | himself |
| Ann Dennett for her house & land | herself |
| Richard Edmunds for Peters Croft | himself |
| William Cooper for his house | Edwd Widgett |

**Professional and commercial residents in the 1798 directory [157]**

*GENTLEMAN*
Penfold Lieut. Peter, Marines
*CLERGY*
Phillips Rev. Edward, Vicar
Whally Rev. Cuthbert, Curate
*PHYSIC*
Bennett John, Surgeon
*TRADERS*
Brookbanks William, (F.) Yeoman
Bushby Robert, Carpenter & Ironmonger
Carter Mary, Carrier
Cutler John, Farmer
Edmunds Richard, (F.) Tallow-chandler and Soap-boiler
Hedgecock Maria, Shopkeeper
Holcombe William, Mercer and Druggist
Markwick John,(F.) Mercer & Grocer
Pain Edward, Yeoman and Fishmonger
Parker Mary, Miller
Penfold John, (F.) Yeoman
Russell John, Post-master
Sayres John,Maltster & Corn-merchant
Shepherd William, (F.) Miller
Tribe William & Son, Maltsters and Corn-merchants
Widgett Edward, Collar-maker

## Houses, their owners and occupiers in the tithe apportionment [158] of 1839

| MAP REF | PRESENT ADDRESS | DESCRIPTION | OWNER | OCCUPIER |
|---|---|---|---|---|
| **High Street** | | | | |
| C1 | Fairoak | Homestead | Luke Sayers | John Barker |
| C2 ) | | House and garden | Luke Sayers | R Parsons |
| C3 ) | | | | |
| C4 | 61 | House and garden | Edward Hollands | self |
| C5 | 57 | House and garden | George Graves | self |
| C6 | 55 | House and garden | Widow Chipper | self |
| C7 | 53 | House and garden | John Weller | Widow Terry |
| C8 | | House and garden | John Weller | Henry Holcombe |
| C9 | | House and garden | John Weller | Streeter |
| C10 | | House and garden | John Weller | Bongard |
| C11 ) | | Barn and yard | John Barker | self |
| C12 ) | | | John Barker | J Paine |
| C13 ) | | Shop and yard | John Barker | William Bushby |
| C14 ) | | | John Barker | William Bushby |
| C15 | | Garden | John Barker | William Bushby |
| C16 | The Vine | House and garden | John Holden | John Burgess |
| C17 | 25 | 2 Cottages&gardens | Susan Loud | Chipper and West |
| C18 | 23 | House and garden | Elizabeth Street | R Hodgkinson |
| C19 | 21 | House &c | John Sayer | C Cook |
| C20 | 19,19a | House and shop | John Sayer | self |
| C22 | 11,13 | Houses & gardens | Jane, Mary, William and Henry Holcombe Catherine Fuller, Ann Marshall and Elizabeth Hewlett | James Burt David Streeter Void |
| C23 | 7,9 Banner House | House stables yard garden &c | William Parker | self |
| C24 | 5 | Storehouse | John Barker | self |
| C25 | 3 | House | John Barker | George Smith and James Parsons |
| C26 | George and Dragon | George Inn & stables | Richard Tamplin | George Winton |
| C27 ) | car | House &c | Richard Tamplin | Void & A Hide |
| C28 ) | park | Storehouse & yard | Mrs Elizabeth Edmunds | Void |
| **Church Road** | | | | |
| C29 ) | | House &c | Mrs Elizabeth Edmunds | J Winchester |
| ) | | | | William Baden |
| C30 ) | 91 | House and shop | Mrs Elizabeth Edmunds | William Cooper |
| C31 ) | to | Garden | Mrs Elizabeth Edmunds | William Cooper |
| C32 ) | 75 | House Bakehouse &c | Rev Peter Crofts | Mrs Stoneham |
| C33 ) | | House garden and shoemakers shop | Laban Bushby | George Long William Sanders |

| *MAP REF* | *PRESENT ADDRESS* | *DESCRIPTION* | *OWNER* | *OCCUPIER* |
|---|---|---|---|---|
| C34 ) | | House yard & shop | Laban Bushby | J Bushby |
| C35 ) | | House and garden | Laban Bushby | Mrs Long |
| C36 | 73 | House and garden | Ann Long | self |
| C37 | 71 | House re building | Joseph & John Moore | )Rebecca Tolley and |
| C38 | 69 | House re building | Elizabeth Curtis Briggs | )Susanna Barnes |
| C39 ) | Church | Rick Yard | Rev Peter Crofts | Thomas Markwick |
| C40 ) | Way | Homestead | Rev Peter Crofts | Thomas Markwick |
| C41 | Church | Church | Parish Officers | |
| C42 | Bowling Green | Garden | Rev Peter Crofts | Thomas Markwick |
| C43 | | Stables waste &c | Rev Peter Crofts | Thomas Markwick |
| C44 | Church House | House and garden | Rev Peter Crofts | Thomas Markwick |
| C45 ) | | Orchard | Rev Peter Crofts | Thomas Markwick |
| C46 ) | | House and stable | George Stringer | self |
| C47 ) | 28 | Cottage | George Stringer | Hazlegrove |
| C48 ) | to | Cottage | George Stringer | W Hart |
| C49 ) | 52 | Cottage and garden | George Stringer | J White |
| C50 ) | | Cottage and garden | George Stringer | J Streeter |
| C51 ) | | House and garden | Henry Floate | Richard Cooper and widow Lambert |
| C52 | 54 | Cottage and garden | Rev Peter Crofts | C Chipper |
| C53 | 56 | Cottage and garden | Rev Peter Crofts | David Hills |
| C54 | 58 | Cottage and garden | Rev Peter Crofts | Thomas Binsted |
| C55 ) | Market | House garden & shops | Philadelphia Cotton | George Stringer |
| C56 ) | House | Cottage | Philadelphia Cotton | John Beech |

**South Street**

| | | | | |
|---|---|---|---|---|
| C57 ) | Priory | Garden, house&garden | Henry Pelling | Lannaway J |
| C58 ) | Close | House | Henry Pelling | Lannaway J |
| C59 ) | | Garden | Henry Pelling | Lannaway J |
| C60 | | House and garden | Thomas Whitby | C Bushby |
| C61 | | Cottage and garden | John Lindup | Charles Bushby |
| C62 | | Cottage and garden | John Lindup | Allen Hide |
| C63 | Pendules | House and garden | Mary Mott | John Collins |
| C64 | Meadow Bank | House and garden | Eliza Street | J Reddefer |
| C65 | | Barn and yard | Richard Penfold | self |
| C66 | | Barn and yard | J Daubuz | Thomas Hill |
| C67a | | Cottage and garden | J Daubuz | Isaac Mitchell |
| C67b | | Cottage and garden | J Daubuz | Edward Stringer |
| C68 | | Cottage and gardens | J Daubuz | Henry Jupp |
| C69 | | House and garden | Soutten Waterman | C Bushby |
| C70 | | Cottage | William Riddles | William Cosens |
| C71 | | Garden | Mary Tribe | John Long |
| C72 | Filling Stn | Pound | Parish Officers | |
| C73 | | Barn and yard | Mary Tribe | self |
| C74 ) | | Barn, stable, coach | Robert Watkins | William Poland |
| C75 ) | | house yard &c | | |

| *MAP REF* | *PRESENT ADDRESS* | *DESCRIPTION* | *OWNER* | *OCCUPIER* |
|---|---|---|---|---|
| C76 | | House and garden | Robert Watkins | Mrs Rudwick |
| C77 | 94,96 | House and garden | Robert Watkins | Edward Elliot |
| C78 | 98 | House and garden | Daniel Monk | self |
| C79 | 100 | House and garden | Thomas Markwick | Charles Roberts |
| C80 | 102,104 | House and garden | William Riddles | self |
| C81 | Park Bldgs | House and garden | Mrs Marian Freeland | Poland |
| C82 | 138 | Garden | John Hide | John Sayers & W Lindup |
| C83 | | Cottage and garden | J Daubuz | Henry Jupp |
| C84 ) | Kingdom Hall | | | R Drewett |
| C85a ) | | House and gardens | Thomas Winton | T Jail |
| C85b ) | | | James Hide | |
| C86 | | Barn and yard | Mary Tribe | self |
| C87 | | Garden | Mary Tribe | Rev J W Warter |
| C88 | | House and garden | Rev J W Warter | self |
| C89 | | Garden | Richard Kent Paine | Rev J W Warter |
| C90 | | House yard and garden | Richard Penfold | Souten Waterman |
| C91 | | Meadow | Richard Penfold | Souten Waterman |
| C92 | | Barn and yard | Richard Penfold | self |
| C93 | | Barn and plat | Richard Penfold | self |
| C94 | Norfolk House | House garden &c | Richard Penfold | self |
| C95 | | House and garden | Richard Penfold | Thomas Dale |
| C96 | Flintstones | Stables and yard | Richard Penfold | self |
| C97 | | Garden | Richard Penfold | self |
| C98 | Bishops Garth | House and garden | Susan Loud | Henry Pelling |
| C99 | | Garden | Rev William Vaux | John Long |
| C100 | | | | |
| C101 | Old Palace | House and garden | Rev William Vaux | Mrs Hill |
| C102 | | Barns croft yard &c | Rev William Vaux | David Sandle |
| C103 | | House and garden | Edward Briggs | self |
| C104 | | Cottage and garden | Henry Pelling | Richard Drewitt |
| C105 | | Cottage and garden | Henry Pelling | Edward Chipper |
| C106 | | Cottage and garden | Henry Pelling | Richard Street |
| C107 | | Cottage and garden | Henry Pelling | R Haybrittle & void |

**High Street**

| | | | | |
|---|---|---|---|---|
| C108 | Post office | House &c | John Pullen | David Sandle |
| C109 | 4 | House and garden | Thomas Whitby | self |
| C110 | 6 | House | James Penfold | Sidney Smith |
| C111 | 8 | Cottage and garden | Sarah Penfold | J Lambert |
| C112 | 10 | Cottage and garden | Sarah Penfold | E Smith |
| C113 | | Cottage and garden | Sarah Penfold | Edward Richardson |
| C114 | 12,14 | Stables yard &c&c | John Pullen | David Sandle |
| C115 | 16 | House and garden | John Bennett | Edward Hide |
| C116 | Gospel Hall | House and yard | as C22 | Widow Streeter |
| C117 | 20 | House and garden | Charles Marshall | J Raison |
| C118 | Chippers Cot | House and garden | Charles Marshall | George Chipper |
| C119 | 24 | House and garden | Charles Marshall | Void |

| MAP REF | PRESENT ADDRESS | DESCRIPTION | OWNER | OCCUPIER |
|---|---|---|---|---|
| C120 | 26 | Castle Inn & premises | Richard Tamplin | J Hide |
| C121 | 28 | Cottage and garden | Selina & Eliza Street | John Duffield |
| C122 | 30 | Cottage and garden | Selina & Eliza Street | William Mitchell |
| C123 | 32 | Cottage and garden | Selina & Eliza Street | George Street |
| C124 | 38 | House and garden | Mary Tribe | Holcombe |
| C125 | 40 | House and garden | Mary Tribe | George Ware |
| C126 | 42 | House and garden | Richard Street | The Misses Street |
| C127 | 44-58 | Meadow | Richard Penfold | self |
| C128 | 60,62 | Shops and garden | Edward Hollands | self |
| C129 | 64,64a | House shop & garden | Stephen Fielder | Jessy Kensett |
| C130 | 66-70 | House and garden | Ann Ware | E Streeter |

**APPENDIX TWO**

# TARRING CLERGY

**Vicars of the parish of West Tarring [159]**

| | |
|---|---|
| 1313 | Richard de Duryngton |
| 1315 | William de Prestone |
| 1316 | Henry de Layton |
| 1320 | Robert de Outon |
| 1357 | Adam de Welde |
| 1357 | Robert de Middleton |
| 1368 | John de Worle |
| 1371 | Stephen de Tallynge |
| 1371 | Robert Balle |
| 1389 | John Esteton |
| 1393 | John Shortere |
| 1417 | John Harptre |
| 1418 | Thomas Symond |
| 1421 | John Shortere |
| 1449 | John Herry |
| 1453 | Roger King |
| 1455 | Nicholas Clifden |
| 1461 | Richard Lybbott |
| 1465 | Nicholas Clyvedon |
| 1476 | Richard Smyth |
| 1496 | Wm Ryngswale |
| 1498 | John New |
| 1510 | Ambrose Medcalf |
| 1515 | John Salter |
| 1516 | John Thompson |
| 1517 | Henry Richardson |
| 1517 | John Oxley |
| 1518 | Simon Oxley |
| 1544 | Nicholas Oxley |
| 1544 | Wm Alanson |
| 1547 | Robert Figgin |
| 1548 | James Bromley |
| 1567 | Thomas Poole |
| 1568 | John Gybbons |
| 1571 | Robert Gybinges |
| 1594 | Robert Evans |
| 1601 | David Evans |
| 1605 | Mark Penkavill MA |
| 1612 | William Tye AM |
| 1621 | John White AM |
| 1638 | William Stanley |
| 1655 | Richard Meggott |
| 1657 | William Pixe |
| 1662 | Edmund Negus |
| 1676 | John Harrison LLD |
| 1697 | Jermanus Dunn AM |
| 1699 | John Gray AM |
| 1699 | Edward Williams AB |
| 1717 | Francis Conduit AB |
| 1720 | David Capon BA |
| 1751 | Thomas Lewis |
| 1766 | Richard Rycroft MA |
| 1786 | Edward Phillips MA |
| 1803 | John Nesbitt Jordan |
| 1819 | Matthew Irving BD |
| 1823 | William Vaux MA |
| 1834 | John Wood Warter MA |
| 1878 | Henry Bailey DD |

*In 1879, the posts of Rector and Vicar were combined*

**Rectors of the parish of West Tarring**

| | |
|---|---|
| c1175 | William the chaplain |
| c1200 | Clerk Master Honor |
| 1257 | Simon of Tarring |
| 1270 | Theodosius de Camill |
| 1282 | Robert de Lacy |
| 1283 | Giles de Andemarde |
| 1288 | Walter de Pecham |
| 1317 | William atte See |
| 1341 | Thos de Hatfeld |
| 1354 | John de Flesco |
| 1354 | John de Borley or Boxleye |
| 1373 | Edward Forest |
| 1373 | John Marchford |
| 1393 | Robert Hallum |
| 1395 | John May |
| 1401 | John Incent |
| 1401 | Roger Bassett LlD |
| 1416 | Roger Heron |
| 1444 | Rd Easton (Lic in Laws) |
| 1449 | Edward Mille |
| 1452 | John Sutton |
| 1480 | John Thwaytes STB |
| 1514 | John Clerke DD |
| 1516 | John Tomson |
| 1517 | John Claymond STB |
| 1532 | Richard Parkehurst AM |
| 1547 | William Bradbridge STB |
| 1570 | John Igulden |
| 1584 | Martin Williams STB |
| 1602 | Benj Charier STP |
| 1614 | Richard Moket STP |
| 1616 | Alex Chapman STP |
| 1629 | John Jeffery STP |
| 1629 | Samuel Bernard STP |
| 1652 | Joseph Mason BD |
| 1660 | William Clewer |
| 1661 | Robert Dale |
| 1672 | John Provost AM |
| 1711 | John Stripe AM |
| 1738 | John Potter MA |
| 1746 | Jeremiah Milles MA |
| 1779 | Richard Milles MA |
| 1845 | The Ecclesiastical Commissioners |
| 1879 | Henry Bailey DD |
| 1892 | Wm Douglas Springett DD |
| 1898 | Charles Lee |
| 1928 | John Godber MA |
| 1949 | Harold H Dyer BA |
| 1958 | James Arthur Rees |
| 1986 | W Edward Jervis |

**Vicars of the chantry of St Mary**

| | |
|---|---|
| 1324 | John de Wymundham |
| 1350 | Robert de Patchying |
| 1353 | Robert Mason |
| 1360 | Stephen de Tallynge |
| 1361 | Martin Tronel |
| 1364 | Robert de Balle |
| 1371 | Thomas Russell |
| 1371 | John Ingram |
| 1374 | Simon Browne |
| 1381 | John Veale |

APPENDIX THREE

# LORDS OF THE MANOR

**Lords of the Manor of West Tarring with Marlpost [160]**

| | |
|---|---|
| c939 | Christ Church Canterbury |
| c1200 | Richard Waleys, Lord of Patching |
| 1209 | Godfrey Waleys, his son |
| ? | Godfrey Waleys, his son |
| c1266 | Richard Waleys, his son |
| 1276 | Christ Church Canterbury |
| 1559 | The Crown |
| c1570 | John Deering |
| c1579 | Edmund Deering, his brother |
| c1610 | Jane Deering |
| 1616 | Sir William Garraway |
| 1626 | Sir Henry Garraway, his son |
| 1646 | William Garraway, his son |
| c1656 | John Garraway, his son |
| 1674 | Thomas Garraway |
| 1700 | Frances Garraway, his widow |
| c1711 | Edward and Richard Norris |
| 1715 | Sir Fisher Tench |
| 1720 | Humphrey Thayer |
| 1723 | Edward Barker |
| c1729 | Edward Barker, his son |
| 1761 | Henry Barker |
| 1775 | Joseph Pickering |
| 1779 | Edward Barker |
| 1835 | Henry John Peachey, Lord Selsey |
| 1838 | James Cuddon |
| 1848 | J U Rastrick |
| 1857 | Henry Rastrick |
| 1869 | |
| 1878 | George Rastrick |
| 1895 | |
| 1914 | Mrs Rastrick |

APPENDIX FOUR

# TARRING STREET NAMES

Many of the names of present day roads and streets in Tarring have historical connotations. Here are some of them:

| | |
|---|---|
| Athelstan Road: | King Athelstan gave the lands of Tarring to the church of Canterbury in the year 939. Ethelwulf and Ethelred Roads are also named after Kings of that period. |
| Barton Close: | This little road stands in the field which was once called the South Barton. |
| Becket Road: | Commemorates St Thomas Becket, Archbishop of Canterbury, and lord of the manor of Tarring from 1162 to 1170. |
| Bishop's Close: | Recalls the association of Tarring with the Archbishop of Canterbury which dates back over a thousand years. |
| Canterbury Road: | One again, commemorating the connection with Canterbury. |
| Castle Road: | Commemorates Chippers Castle, the flint cottage now known as Chippers Cottage. |
| Chantry Road: | Named after the chantry of St Mary, attached to Tarring church between the thirteenth and sixteenth centuries. |
| Chippers Road: | Named after the Chipper family, associated with Tarring for over three hundred years. |
| Church Road: | Earlier called Church Lane, this path has linked the church to the Old Palace and the market-place for at least eight hundred years. |
| Glebe Road: | Stands on the glebe lands of Tarring rectory. |
| Haynes Road: | The old thatched cottage which was demolished to make way for Rectory Road was called The Haynes, or Haynes Cottage, after Thomas and Love Haynes, who once lived there. |
| Highfield Road: | Recalls the name of the house on the east of Rectory Road, and the farm which once surrounded it. |
| Lanfranc Road: | Lanfranc was Archbishop of Canterbury, and lord of the manor of Tarring, from 1070 to 1089. |
| Lincett Avenue: | Lincett barn stood near here. |

| | |
|---|---|
| Mill Road: | Mill Road runs across the site of the great Heene field, where a windmill stood between 1587 and 1903. |
| Northfield Road: | Northfield, where this road now stands, was one of the three great open fields of Tarring. The others were Southfield to the south, and the Townfield in the middle. |
| Parkfield Road: | The old peoples' home now called The Priory was originally called Parkfield, and this road was named after it. |
| Peverel Road: | The village is often called West Tarring to distinguish it from another Sussex village, Tarring Neville, near Newhaven. The manor of Tarring Peverel was situated there, but the name Peverel has often been wrongly attributed to our village by historians in the past. |
| Rectory Road: | Named after the Tarring rectory which stood on the site of Tarring Gate, and was demolished to make way for the road. |
| St Andrews Road: | The saint to whom the parish church has long been dedicated. |
| St Anselms Road: | St Anselm was Archbishop of Canterbury, and lord of the manor of Tarring, from 1093 to 1109. |
| St Dunstans Road: | The patron saint of Sussex, St Dunstan was Archbishop of Canterbury, and lord of the manor of Tarring, from 960 to 988. |
| St Thomas's Road: | Again, recalling St Thomas Becket. |
| South Street: | This road has been called the south street of Tarring since as early as 1650. |
| Terringes Avenue: | Terringes was an early name for Tarring. |
| Twitten Way: | Named after the narrow footpath, called a twitten in Sussex, which it follows. |

APPENDIX FIVE

# THE MILLER'S TOMB

The inscriptions on the tomb of John Oliver, the miller of Highdown, recorded [161] in 1805, just twelve years after the tomb was finally occupied.

'Upon the top of the Tomb I found the following record:

> *For the reception of the body of John Oliver, when deceased, to the will of God; granted by William Westbrook Richardson, Esq. 1776*
>
> *As in Adam all die, so in Christ shall all be made alive. 1 Cor. xv. 22.*
>
> *The law came by Moses; but grace and truth by Jesus Christ. John i. 17.*
>
> *God so loved the world, that he gave his only begotten Son, that whosoever believeth in him shall not perish, but have everlasting life.*
> *John iii. 15.*
>
> *Wherefore I perceive that there is nothing better than that a man should rejoice in his own works, for that is his portion; for who shall bring him to see what shall be after him. Eccles. iii. 22.*
>
> *Knowing that shortly I must put off this my earthly tabernacle, even as our Lord Jesus Christ hath shewed me. 2 Peter, i. 14.*

At the west end there are two figures, *Time* and *Death* - encircled with these two passages

> *The fear of the Lord is the beginning of wisdom; but to keep his commandments is holiness to the Lord.*

Then follow these lines -

*Death why so fast - pray stop your hand,*
*And let my glass run out its sand;*
*As neither death nor time will stay,*
*Let us improve the present day.*
*Why start you at this skeleton -*
*'Tis your own picture which you shun;*
*Alive it did resemble thee,*
*And thou, when dead, like that shall be;*
*But tho' death must have his will,*
*Yet, old time prolongs the date*
*Till the measure we shall fill*
*That's allotted us by fate;*
*When that's done - then Time and Death*
*Both agree to take our breath!*

On the opposite or eastern end are these apologetic lines -

*Why should my fancy anyone offend,*
*Whose good or ill does not on it depend;*
*'Tis at my own expense, except the land,*
*A generous grant on which my tomb doth stand;*
*This is the only spot that I have chose*
*Wherein to take my lasting long repose;*
*Here in the dust my body lieth down,*
*You'll say it is not consecrated ground -*
*I grant the same, but where shall we ere find*
*The spot that ere can purify the mind;*
*Nor to the body any lustre give,*
*This more depends on what a life we live:*
*For when the trumpet shall begin to sound*
*T'will not avail e'en where the body's found!*

Lastly, on the side as you enter the field, is,

*In Memory*
*of JOHN OLIVER, Miller,*
*who departed this life,*
*the 22d of April 1793,*
*aged 84 years.*

APPENDIX SIX

# A STORY OF ST THOMAS BECKET

The following article appeared in the Worthing Monthly Record and District Chronicle for October 2nd, 1854. From its style and content, it is unlikely to be authentic, but it is certainly well researched and there may be some element of truth in it.

Dryasdust was a regular columnist in the newspaper at the time.

## AN UNPUBLISHED INCIDENT IN THE LIFE OF THOMAS Á BECKET.

– Communicated by Dryasdust, Jun

How the following MS fell into our hands is of little moment. That it should so long have escaped the researches of the several learned biographers of Á BECKET is a circumstance for their readers to enquire into, not for us to account for. So far as the character of the monkish latin in which it is written is evidence, it would appear to be of the date of the twelfth, or beginning of the thirteenth century. It is subscribed Iohannes Hen, - or as it is now written, Heene - where was a cell of the House of the Holy Trinity established at Arundel, and of which he was probably a brother.

The fragment is headed

*Seyncte Thomas of Canterburie at his Manor-house of Terrings, in the Year of Grace, MCLXXI*

Moth and mildew have done for the writer what weary readers often do for more modern wielders of the stylus - lopped off the beginning and the end of the narration, so that it is necessary to glean a few introductory particulars from such not wholly obliterated lines as these literary pilferers have left us.

The subject is an incident that occurred to the Archbishop at the Old Manor House at Tarring, whither he was accustomed to betake himself from the heats and strifes of Lambeth, in his latter years.

The scene appears to open in the refectory: the hour to be the noonday meal: the company the Prelate, Father Anselmo his almoner, who had followed in his grace's train from Italy; Hubert, Pryor of a neighbouring Monastery, whose character is preserved in two or three legible lines as one who had "as curious a judgement in a stoup of good ale as his lordship's pantler himself", and a throng of ecclesiastics which a dispenser of so many good things as a lord primate never failed to attract, and among them it may be assumed our chronicler had a place.

All these appear to have been seated round the board, at the head of which sat the great man himself; but animated with no genial spirit, for these were the troublous times that preceded his martyrdom, and the coming shadow was already falling upon him.

The manuscript here becomes legible.

*' "—" said Prior Hubert, desirous of distracting my lord from his sad thought- "As Father Anselmo and I walked in the orchard yonder at noon, for the shadow of the rare trees your grace brought hither from Italy, our conversation was broken in upon by the song of a bird, which Anselmo says he has not heard since he left his own country." "Il Beccafico" - interjected the Italian. "Is it possible," said my lord, "that this little creature can have traversed the rough seas to seek out the fruit of that rare plant you mention?" "It is sooth your grace, by an infallible sign; for lo, it hath stirred up such savory memories of the dainty pasties of St. Jerome of the Campagna in Anselmo, that he hath no stomach for the plain english fare of your grace's board."*

*The Italian looked not pleasantly on this sally of our good Pryor; but my lord's thoughts were wandering far away, and he heeded nothing of the idle jesting, which, indeed, he did ever discourage. Presently he arose from table and with hasty steps passed to the door, through the garden, and so by the wicket into the Teintes, where he was wont to take the air. Like wildfire the news ran through the hamlet, "the Archbishop is abroad." The smith left his forge and the franklin his team, and all, men and women, old and young, hurried to the scene of his grace's walk, for he was used to give a pleasant word to all he met; and moreover he scattered alms with no niggard hand.*

*But now not a benedicite greeted the most faithful of his flock, nor a silver groat fell to the most needy, but with a quick step and frowning brow he strode through the assembled villagers, clutching his staff the while as though he was using it as a rod for his enemies.*

*Thereat the throng stood aloof, for yet fresh in men's mouths was the story of the strange mishap that had befallen the men of Stroud, who spitefully severing a useful member of the Archbishop's horse, as he was journeying through their town, did unexpectedly find themselves endowed, in their own persons, with the same caudal appendage.**

*All stood aside, save only one - Mad Peg of Dorrington, as she was used to be called. Half bent with age, her dark eyes just peering above the head of her staff through the grey locks that hung in uncomely fashion over her face, she stood full in the path. My lord little heeded the apparition, till a shrill voice which startled all ears, recalled his wandering faculties.*

*"Beware!" it said, "beware of your steps! wicked men are on your track: your winding sheet is weaving, and there's blood in the woof."*

*At these words consternation seized upon us; but my lord was troubled most of all. Yet after a while, when the rustics would have laid hands on her, and a cry arose "to the cucking stool!" and they were hurrying her away to the pond that stood by the lytch gate of the Church yard where Lucky Long had been drowned for a witch the year preceding, my lord desired them to forbear; which indeed was over-rash for his grace - but he was ever pitiful - for she looked a villainous witch of Endor.'*

The outer leaves of the manuscript again become illegible, which is the less important as it appears the writer only proceeds to relate the accomplishment of the prediction in the murder of the Archbishop before the high altar at Canterbury in the succeeding Christmas, all of which is matter of common history.

* Our Chronicler is singularly authenticated by Polydore Virgil, who wrote three centuries after. - Vide Urb. Angel. Hist. fol.218.

# REFERENCES

**Abbreviations used in all references**

| | |
|---|---|
| BL | British Library |
| PRO | Public Record Office |
| SAC | Sussex Archaeological Collections |
| SNQ | Sussex Notes and Queries |
| SRS | Sussex Record Society |
| VCH | The Victoria History of the County of Sussex |
| WRL | Worthing Reference Library |
| WSRO | West Sussex Record Office |

**Introduction**

1 Topographical Miscellanies 1792
2 SRS lvii
3 SNQ viii p 106
4 SAC xxxviii
5 WSRO additional manuscripts 106-115
6 PRO IR 30/35/260
7 Lay Subsidy Roll 258/14 14 Chas II, transcribed by Sayers in WRL
8 WSRO

**Chapter 1**

9 Historic Manuscripts Commission 80, Sackville (Knole) i, p 84
10 John Taylor, The Honourable and Memorable Foundations, 1636
11 William Cooper, Smuggling in Sussex, 1858, for this and subsequent details
12 Sussex Weekly Advertiser, 14 March 1763
13 J W Warter, The Seaboard and the Down, 1860
14 L Candlin, Tales of Old Sussex, 1986
15 F W H Migeod, Worthing, A Survey, 1938

**Chapter 2**

16 SAC cii p11
17 ibid p12
18 SRS vii p43
19 Chronicles of Holinshed, 1586
20 Worthing Herald, 29 September 1971
21 Worthing Herald, 11 February 1972, Worthing Guardian, 6 August 1987
22 Worthing Herald, 8 March 1933

23 Worthing Gazette, 20 October 1971
24 F W H Migeod, Worthing, a Survey, 1938
25 Universal British Directory, 1798
26 Revd E Boys Ellman, Recollections of a Sussex Parson, 1925

**Chapter 3**

27 J Evans, Worthing, 1805
28 J W Warter, The Seaboard and the Down, 1860
29 Worthing Gazette, 9 June 1925

**Chapter 4**

30 BL Sloane manuscripts 4025 f224-238
31 Goodman collection WRL
32 SNQ xi p164
33 Universal British Directory, 1798
34 Worthing Herald, 13 January 1956
35 Worthing Herald, 20 January 1956

**Chapter 5**

36 BL add manuscript 38487
37 J Evans, Worthing, 1805
38 F Fox-Wilson, The Story of Goring and Highdown, 1987
39 Rachael Burtenshaw's will, WSRO
40 Census 1851
41 Worthing Herald, 8 March 1933
42 Worthing Herald, 4 September 1959
43 ditto, 22 January 1972
44 W Cobbett, Rural Rides, 1830
45 L Candlin, Tales of Old Sussex, 1986
46 Universal British Directory, 1798
47 H Smail, The Worthing Road and its Coaches, 1944
48 ibid
49 Worthing Gazette, 13 November 1957

**Chapter 6**

50 Quarter Sessions' Order Book, Chichester, Easter, 1642, SRS liv
51 J W Warter, The Seaboard and the Down, 1860
52 Worthing Herald, 5 July 1958
53 SAC cii p10
54 Worthing Gazette, 14 December 1927, SAC lxxiv p210, SAC xli p69,72
55 Accounts, receipts and payments, 20 Henry VII, 1504-6, Lambeth Palace Library as quoted by Sayers in an unpublished manuscript in WRL
56 WSRO Ep IV/8/24
57 Goodman Collection, WRL

58 Worthing Herald, 29 September 1971
59 Worthing Gazette, 14 December 1927
60 Goodman Collection, WRL
61 SAC ci p28-34

**Chapter 7**

62 J R Armstrong, A History of Sussex, 1984
63 Caesar, the Conquest of Gaul, Penguin, 1951
64 K Branigan, Roman Britain, 1980
65 SNQ xi p161
66 F W H Migeod, Worthing, A Survey, 1938
67 Ordnance Survey map of Roman Britain
68 J Glover, The Place Names of Sussex, 1975
69 The Anglo Saxon Chronicle, Chronicles and Memorials of Great Britain and Ireland, 1861
70 SAC lxxxviii p53
71 Domesday book
72 Topographical Miscellanies, 1792
73 VCH v2 p107
74 SNQ viii p106, Sayers, Transcriptions of Records of the Past, 1903
75 see for example R Budgen, An Actual Survey of the County of Sussex, 1724, and Cartwright, History of the Rape of Bramber, 1830
76 A F Hughes, The Archbishop's Palace West Tarring, a short history, 1987
77 Calendar of Patent Rolls, 1277
78 Modern prices courtesy of Shannon Meats and Tarring Corn Stores, South St Tarring
79 SRS lvii
80 Miscellaneous Inquisitions, 1397
81 WSRO Ep IV/8/24
82 Topographical Miscellanies, 1792
83 J W Warter, Parochial Fragments, 1853
84 SAC vol cii
85 Worthing Gazette, 14 December 1927; Sayers notes in WRL
86 PRO IR 20/35/260
87 J W Warter, Parochial Fragments, 1853, p238
88 Ordnance Survey map, 1898

**Chapter 8**

89 PRO IR 30/35/260
90 Ordnance Survey maps, 1875, 1898
91 SAC cii pp 12-27
92 WSRO Ep IV/8/24
93 Topographical Miscellanies, 1792
94 Worthing Herald, 15 September 1972
95 J Watts, Old Worthing As I Remember It, 1982
96 Worthing Teachers Centre, A History of Worthing, 1976
97 F W H Migeod, Worthing, A Survey, 1938
98 Sussex Weekly Advertiser, 23 May 1803

**Chapter 9**


99 E Cartwright, History of the Rape of Bramber, 1830
100 A M Rowland & T P Hudson, A History of Worthing, 1983, p 76
101 A facsimile of the original charter, with the seal, can be seen at the Parsonage Restaurant, and a transcription in the Calendar of Charter Rolls, 1427-1516, 40. Translations have been published in the West Sussex Gazette, 22 March 1866, and this one, by Edward Sayers, in the Worthing Gazette for 18 January 1905
102 Shearsmith, A Topographical Description of Worthing, 1821
103 Star Chamber Proceedings, SRS xvi p81
104 E Sayers, unpublished manuscript in WRL
105 M Bassett, The Hentys, 1954
106 Worthing Herald, 24 March 1967, Worthing Gazette, 7 June 1967


**Chapter 10**


107 Bede, A History of the English Church and People
108 SAC lxxxvi p82
109 SAC lxxxvi p100
110 VCH i p389
111 Topographical Miscellanies, 1792
112 L F Salzman, The Chartulary of the Priory of St Peter at Sele, 1923
113 W Victor Cook, The Story of Sussex, 1920
114 F W H Migeod, Worthing, A Survey, 1938
115 SRS lxxiv
116 SNQ vi p68
117 Assize Roll 909A, 33 Henry III, 1249, quoted in Worthing Survey
118 SAC xcv, (King's Bench Controlment Roll 18, m 21d)
119 SRS lxxiv
120 SNQ iv p230
121 G M Trevelyan, Illustrated English Social History, 1949-52
122 SNQ iii,iv
123 SNQ iv p110
124 E Sayers, Transcriptions of Records of the Past, 1903
125 ibid
126 SNQ iii p21
127 E Sayers, unpublished manuscript in WRL
128 The Parish Church of Saint Andrew, West Tarring, A Short History, for this and subsequent information
129 The Worthing Monthly Record and District Chronicle, 1 May 1854
130 ibid, 1 December 1854
131 The Worthing Monthly Record and District Chronicle, 1 June 1855


**Chapter 11**


132 J W Warter, Parochial Fragments, 1853
133 Worthing Intelligencer, 26 January 1884
134 M A Lower (ed), A Survey of the Coast of Sussex made in 1587, 1870

135 A Mee, Sussex in Explanation, quoted in the Worthing Herald, 17 August 1956
136 Worthing Gazette, 7 January 1957
137 M Frost, The Early History of Worthing, 1929
138 W Victor Cook, The Story of Sussex, 1920
139 J Dallaway and E Cartwright, History of Sussex, 1815-1832
140 R Budgen, An Actual Survey of the County of Sussex, 1724
141 J W Warter, Parochial Fragments, 1853, p270
142 ibid
143 J Mackoull, A Sketch of Worthing, 1817
144 E Cartwright, History of the Rape of Bramber, 1830
145 J W Warter, Parochial Fragments, 1853, p61
146 E Sayers, Transcriptions of Records of the Past, 1903
147 Worthing Gazette, 5 December 1979

**Appendices**

148 SRS lvii
149 SRS x
150 ibid
151 SRS lvi
152 SNQ vii
153 BL Lansdowne ms 784
154 SRS v
155 Lay Subsidy Roll 258/14 14 Chas II, transcribed by Sayers in WRL
156 WSRO
157 Universal British Directory, 1798
158 PRO IR 29,30/35/260
159 Compiled from records mainly in WSRO. The list agrees broadly with that displayed in the church. The reference to Clerk Master Honor is in Migeod's Worthing Survey.
160 Compiled from the Victoria County History and the manor court rolls
161 J Evans, A Picture of Worthing, 1805

# BIBLIOGRAPHY


**The Local Area**

| | |
|---|---|
| J Evans | A Picture of Worthing, 1805 |
| F Fox-Wilson | The Story of Goring and Highdown, 1987 |
| M Frost | The Early History of Worthing, 1929 |
| A F Hughes | The Archbishop's Palace West Tarring, a short history, 1987 |
| F W H Migeod (ed) | Worthing, a Survey of Times Past and Present, 1938 |
| A M Rowland & T P Hudson | A History of Worthing, 1983, an extract from the Victoria County History of Sussex, 1980 |
| E Sayers (ed) | Transcripts of, and Extracts from, Records of the Past, 1903 |
| H Smail | The Worthing Map Story, 1949 |
| H Smail | The Worthing Road and its Coaches, 1944 |
| H Smail & others | Worthing Parade, vols 1,2, 1951, 1954 |
| J W Warter | Parochial Fragments relating to the Parish of West Tarring, 1853 |
| J W Warter | My Parish, the Seaboard and the Down, 1860 |
| J Watts | Old Worthing As I Remember It, 1982 |
| Anon | The Parish Church of Saint Andrew, West Tarring, A Short History |

**Sussex**

| | |
|---|---|
| J R Armstrong | A History of Sussex,1984 |
| E Boys Ellman | Recollections of a Sussex Parson, 1912 |
| E Cartwright | A History of the Rape of Bramber, 1830 |
| W Victor Cook | The Story of Sussex, 1920 |

**General**

| | |
|---|---|
| G M Trevelyan | Illustrated English Social History, 4 vols, 1949-52 |

# INDEX

The many Tarring people listed in Appendices 1-3 have not been indexed individually.